BrightRED Study Guide

Curriculum for Excellence

N4

ENGLISH

Sheena Greco

First published in 2015 by:
Bright Red Publishing Ltd
1 Torphichen Street
Edinburgh
EH3 8HX

A CIP record for this book is available from the British Library

ISBN 978-1-906736-49-1

With thanks to:
PDQ Digital Media Solutions Ltd (layout), Sue Moody, Bright Writing Ltd. (copy-edit)

Cover design and series book design by Caleb Rutherford – e i d e t i c

Acknowledgements
Permission has been sought from all relevant copyright holders and Bright Red Publishing are grateful for the use of the following:

Oorka/Dreamstime.com (8, 81, 91, 92); An extract from 'The Lighthouse' in 'Agnes Owens: The Complete Short Stories' by Agnes Owens, Polygon, 2008. Reproduced by permission of Birlinn Ltd. www.birlinn.co.uk (p 9); An article from http://www.bbc.co.uk/news/uk-scotland-glasgow-west-25087376 © BBC News (p 9); Brian A Jackson/Shutterstock.com (p 10); Karin Muller/freeimages.com (p 12); Image © Fraser Doherty (p 12); An extract from http://www.newbusiness.co.uk/articles/entrepreneurs/fraser-doherty-how-i-set-superjam © New Business/Fraser Doherty (pp 12-13); ginosphoto/iStock.com (p 13); Ami Parikh/Shutterstock.com (p 14); Image © Fraser Doherty (p 15); Advert for Arran on a Plate © Chris Attkins (p 16); Image © Fraser Doherty (p 17); Roman_Gorielov/iStock.com (p 18); Artwork from 'Wonder' © Tad Carpenter. Reproduced by arrangement with The Random House Group Ltd. (p 19); Artwork from 'Freak the Mighty' by permission of Usborne Publishing, 83-85 Saffron Hill, London EC1N 8RT, UK. www.usborne.com. Copyright © 2008 Usborne Publishing Ltd (p 19); Davide Guglielmo/freeimages.com (p 20); An extract from 'Wonder' by R.J. Palacio, published by Random House, Inc © 2012 R.J. Palacio (p 20); An extract from 'Freak the Mighty' by Rodman Philbrick, published by Usborne Publishing Ltd © 1993 Rodman Philbrick (p 21); NAR studio/Shutterstock.com (p 22); 3 photos by Caleb Rutherford e i d e t i c (pp 23 & 24); The poem Guid Taste from www.Scottishpoetrylibrary.org.uk/poetry/poems/guid-taste. Thanks to Suruchi Restaurants and Scottish Language Dictionaries (p 25); JoeGough/iStock.com (p 26); Caleb Rutherford e i d e t i c (p 27); Pete Souza (public domain) (p 28); An article from https://www.dailywhat.org.uk/2014/01/cats-may-get-jobs-in-westminster.aspx © Herald & Times Group (p 28); michaeljung/iStock.com (p 30); tifonimages/iStock.com (p 30); Lush/Dreamstime.com (p 31); H Matthew Howarth (CC BY-SA 2.0)1 (p 32); An extract from 'Of Mice and Men' by John Steinbeck. Published by Penguin Books © 1937 John Steinbeck (p 32); An article from https://www.dailywhat.org.uk/2014/01/branding-matters.aspx © Herald & Times Group (p 34); Jieyu Lai/Dreamstime.com (p 34); monkeybusinessimages/iStock.com (p 35); Caleb Rutherford e i d e t i c (p 36); Marjan Lazarevski (CC BY-ND 2.0)2 (p 37); Vasaleks/Shutterstock.com (p 37); Aleksandr Bryliaev/Shutterstock.com (p 37); AlexandreNunes/Shutterstock.com (p 38); Prillfoto/Dreamstime.com (p 38); fabervisum/iStock.com (p 39); Caleb Rutherford e i d e t i c (p 39); Gemenacom/Dreamstime.com (p 40); Les Haines (CC BY 2.0)3 (p 41); Rbohdan (CC BY-SA 3.0)4 (p 41); Caleb Rutherford e i d e t i c (p 42); FrankRamspott/iStock.com (p 43); John D. and Catherine T. MacArthur Foundation (CC BY 4.0)5 (p 44); Greg Epperson/Dreamstime.com (p 44); Helga Esteb/Shutterstock.com (p 46); Michal Zacharzewski/freeimages.com (p 47); Leigh Prather/Dreamstime.com (p 50); shironosov/iStock.com (p 51); michael lorenzo/freeimages.com (p 51); petrograd99/iStock.com (p 52); freefoodphotos.com (CC BY 3.0)6 (p 53); Palto/Dreamstime.com (p 55); Robert Doucette (p 56); Extract from 'The Runaway' by Katie Flynn, published by Arrow books, The Random House Group Limited © 2012 (p 59); Davide Guglielmo/freeimages.com, Caleb Rutherford e i d e t i c (p 59); Fredredhat/Dreamstime.com (p 60, 61, 66); lanych/iStock.com (p 61); Semnoz (CC BY-SA 3.0)4 (p 61); A Case of Murder' by Vernon Scannell from 'New and Collected Poems 1950–1993' Published by Faber & Faber © The Vernon Scannell Estate (p 62); Lulamej/Dreamstime.com (p 62); Caleb Rutherford e i d e t i c (p 63); scyther5/iStock.com (p 64); Maksym Bondarchuk/Dreamstime.com (p 65); frentusha and Tsyhun/iStock.com (p 66); Alptraum/Dreamstime.com (p 67); An etxract from 'Scotland's Stories of Home Learning resources CFE Levels Early – 4 and Senior Phase' © Chris Leslie/Scottish Book Trust (p 67); GlobalP/iStock.com (p 67); Vjeran Lisjak/freeimages.com (p 68); The article 'The Day After The Music Died' by eter McHugh, taken from http://www.bbc.co.uk/radioscotland/dayslikethis/stories/the_day_after_the_music_died.shtml © BBC/Peter McHugh/Scottish Book Trust (p 68); huePhotography/iStock.com (p 69); skodonnell/iStock.com (p 70); The poster 'What Cyclists Would Like Motorists to Know. Department of Transport 1998 © Crown Copyright. Contains public sector information licensed under the Open Government Licence v3.0 (p 70); Elma (CC BY 2.0)3 (p 71); Jstone/Shutterstock.com (p 71); Marcel-Jan Krijgsman/freeimages.com (p 72); Neil A. Armstrong/NASA (p 73); Marshall Astor (CC BY 2.0)3 (p 74); fazon1/iStock.com (p 75); Steve Jurvetson (CC BY 2.0)3 (p 75); David Schroeter (CC BY-ND 2.0)2 (p 76); Dave Edmonds/freeimages.com (p 77); A letter from Jenni Herd reproduced in the The Times: http://www.thetimes.co.uk/tto/opinion/letters/article4021903.ece Reproduced by permission of Jenni Herd (p 77); Andy Dean Photography/Shutterstock.com (p 78); graja/Shutterstock.com (p 79); xavigm/iStock.com (p 80); Andrey_Popov/iStock.com (p 82); Extract taken from 'The Steamie', by Tony Roper. Play text published in Scot-free: New Scottish Plays, edited by Alasdair Cameron (Nick Hern Books, 1990). Excerpted with permission of Nick Hern Books Ltd: www.nickhernbooks.co.uk (p 84); TheWhiteHat (CC BY-SA 3.0)4 (p 85); Shalom Tesciuba (p 85); Luissantos84/Dreamstime.com (p 85); Nana B Agyei (CC BY 2.0)3 (p 86); andreusK/iStock.com (p 86); The poem 'Unrelated Incidents – No.3' by Tom Leonard. Reproduced by permission of Tom Leonard (p 88); Sergey Nivens/Shutterstock.com (p 88); Liam Quinn (CC BY-SA 2.0)1 (p 89); epSos.de (CC BY 2.0)3 (p 89); K. Kendall (CC BY 2.0)3 (p 89); Lilyana Vynogradova/iStock.com (p 89); Steven Straiton (CC BY 2.0)3 (p 90); Pixelrobot/Dreamstime.com (p 90); Nicolas Raymond (CC BY 2.0)3 (p 91); tetmc/iStock.com (p 93); jaylopez/freeimages.com (p 94); Caleb Rutherford e i d e t i c (p 95); Pablo Scapinachis/shutterstock (p 96); cookelma/iStock.com (p 98); Borusikk/Dreamstime.com (p 101); Jonathan Ross/Dreamstime.com (p 102); Zsuzsa N.K./freeimages.com (p 103); Ludmila Lemke/Dreamstime.com (p 104); lovleah/iStock.com (p 105).

Printed and bound in the UK by Charlesworth Press

CONTENTS

NATIONAL 4 ENGLISH STUDY GUIDE

INTRODUCTION

KEY SKILL – READING

KEY SKILL – LISTENING

KEY SKILL – WRITING

KEY SKILL – TALKING

THE ADDED VALUE UNIT

APPENDICES

INTRODUCTION

THE NATIONAL 4 ENGLISH COURSE

The National 4 English Course will develop your skills in reading, listening, writing and talking. These skills are vital – whatever your future holds. In this chapter we're going to look at the structure of the course, the skills it will help you to develop and the texts you will read, watch and create in the process.

COURSE STRUCTURE

The National 4 English Course contains four units. These units are:

- Analysis and Evaluation unit – this unit is about understanding language (reading and listening)
- Creation and Production unit – this unit is about using language (writing and talking)
- Literacy Unit – this unit is about understanding and using language (reading, listening, writing and talking)
- Added Value Unit – this unit is an assignment that includes all four skills – reading, writing, talking and listening

ONLINE

There is more information about the National 4 English Course and Units at www.sqa.org.uk

The table below gives you more information about these units. Reading, listening, writing and talking are equally important in National 4 English.

Name of unit	Skills	Unit content	Examples of learning activities
Analysis and Evaluation	Understanding language	This unit helps you to develop your listening and reading skills. You will learn how to understand, analyse and evaluate spoken and written texts.	-Listening to a podcast -Reading a poem -Listening to an advertisement -Reading a web page
Creation and Production	Using language	This unit helps you to develop your writing and talking skills. You will learn how to create written texts and how to talk individually and in a pair/group.	-Writing a report -Giving an individual talk -Writing a letter -Discussing in a group
Literacy	Understanding and using language	This unit helps you to develop your reading, listening, writing and talking skills. You will learn how to understand, analyse and evaluate spoken and written texts. You will learn how to create written texts and how to talk individually and in a pair/group.	-Listening to a radio programme -Reading a leaflet -Writing an article -Interviewing a partner
Added Value	Understanding and using language	This unit helps you to develop and apply your reading, listening, writing and talking skills.	-Reading two poems and writing/ talking about them

SKILLS FOR LEARNING, LIFE AND WORK

Of course, you will develop lots of other useful skills as you work through National 4 English, such as:

participating
communicating
discussing
organising
studying
revising
researching
using IT

collaborating
thinking
contributing
summarising
reporting
responding
word-processing

 **ACTIVITY**

Discuss with your partner which of the above skills is most useful to you at the moment. For example, if you have a paper round, communicating with your customers might be the most important skill. Or if you are involved in a local community group, then collaboration will be important.

A WORD ABOUT TEXTS...

You will develop your language skills in N4 English 'in the contexts of literature, language and media'. This means that you will read, watch and create lots of different texts. These could be print, digital or media texts, and they could be fiction or non-fiction texts.

In this Study Guide, we will define these texts as follows:

Type of text	Definition	Examples
Print text	A written (or printed) text which contains words (and possibly images)	-A novel – for example, *The Book Thief* by Markus Zusak -A printed newspaper -A postcard
Digital text	An online version of a written (or printed) text – for example, a text read or seen on a smart phone or computer which contains words (and possibly images)	-An online poem – for example, *Out, Out* by Robert Frost at www.poemhunter.com -A text message -A Facebook page
Media text	A text using words and/or sounds and/or images and/or film clips and/or interactive features	-A film – for example, *Up* -A TV advertisement -A video game – for example, *Professor Layton and the Curious Village* -A magazine – for example, *TV Times*

 **ACTIVITY:** Which Text?

Look at the table above. Can you think of some more examples for each type of text?

Now share your ideas with a partner. Look at page 6 for information about 'learning together' with partners or small groups. What examples have you chosen? Be prepared to share your ideas with the rest of the group/class.

 ONLINE

Check out the website http://www.timeincuk.com/about/ where you will find lots of examples of magazines – for example, *Mountain Bike Rider.* Why not design your own magazine cover based on one of the examples on the web page?

 **ACTIVITY:** Print, Digital or Media?

Look at the list of texts below. Decide whether you think the text could be print, digital and/or media and put a tick in the appropriate box. For example, a recipe could be both a print text (a recipe **book**) and a digital text (a cookery **website**). Discuss your list with your partner. Be prepared to share your ideas with the rest of your group/class.

Type of text	Print	Digital	Media
Recipe	✓	✓	
Travel writing			
Textbook			
Song lyrics			
Instructions			
Wiki			
Timetable			
Letter			
Blog			
Comic			
Application form			

 THINGS TO DO AND THINK ABOUT

Why not keep a language diary? For a whole day, note down every time you use or understand language. This means noting everything you read and write, starting from the moment you wake up. You will be surprised at the amount of language you come across and use every day! Look at Kirsty's language diary below to help you get started.

 ONLINE

Look at the 'Readaxation Diary' at http://www.nicolamorgan.com/wp-content/uploads/2014/05/MyReadaxationDiary.pdf. Keeping a diary like this for seven days is a fun way of finding out if reading reduces stress!

Time	Understanding language	Using language
7.20	Read cereal packet	
7.30	Read text from Haley	
7.32		Wrote text to Haley
7.45	Read bus stop timetable	
7.48	Read advertisement on side of bus	
7.50	Read text from Haley	
7.55		Wrote text to Haley
8.00	Read free newspaper...	
8.05		Wrote text to mum...

HOW TO USE THIS STUDY GUIDE

HOW THIS BOOK IS ORGANISED

As you work through this Study Guide, you will develop each of the four language skills – reading, listening, writing and talking. Each chapter will focus on one of these skills, although the activities will help you to develop the other language skills at the same time. So, for example, to help you to write creatively, you'll be asked to read some creative writing. To help you to participate effectively in a group discussion, you'll be asked to listen, too. These are called 'integrated' activities and they will be clearly explained to you as you work through the Guide.

ASSESSMENT

To pass the National 4 English Course, you have to pass all four units. National 4 English is internally assessed. This means that you will do these assessments in your school or college, usually in a classroom situation. To gain an overall award, you have to pass all the units of the course. To pass, you need to show the assessor that you can read, listen, write and talk at National 4 level. The assessor will be someone you know such as your teacher.

LEARNING TOGETHER

When you learn individually, you are learning on your own. When you discuss your ideas with a partner or in a group, you are learning together.

When you learn together, you:

- rely on and help each other
- are all responsible for the completion of the task
- work together by trusting each other
- evaluate your work and set targets for yourselves
- communicate with each other.

When there is a pair or group activity in this book, you will see the heading **Learning together** with the icon above. These 'Learning together' activities usually ask you to work on your own, then work with a partner/group. This will help you learn and will also help you to develop your communication and team-making skills.

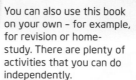

DON'T FORGET

You can also use this book on your own – for example, for revision or home-study. There are plenty of activities that you can do independently.

REVIEWING YOUR LEARNING

At the end of each chapter, you will be asked to think about what/how you have learned. You could also identify things that you can do well and things that you want to improve. Ask yourself the following questions:

- What three key things have you learned from this chapter?
- What aspects of the chapter did you find challenging, if any?
- What aspects of the chapter did you find easy, if any?
- What did you enjoy about this chapter?
- What did you not enjoy?
- What might improve your learning next time?
- Any other comments on your learning?

AND FINALLY ...

Each unit in the National 4 English Course contains **Outcomes** and **Assessment Standards**. Let's look in more detail at what these are.

EXAMPLE

Here's an example of an **Outcome** from the Literacy Unit. The 'Outcome' is the skill you will develop. In this case, the Outcome is to show that you can write texts accurately (at National 4 level). The '**Assessment Standards**' are what you have to do to show you have this skill. So, to show you can write accurate texts (at National 4 level) you have to use appropriate language, organise your writing, and use spelling, punctuation and grammar to make your writing clear.

	Literacy Unit
Outcome	3. Write straightforward technically accurate texts by:
Assessment Standards	3.1 Selecting and using appropriate straightforward language 3.2 Organising writing appropriately 3.3 Using appropriate spelling, punctuation and grammar

The Outcomes and Assessment Standards for each skill are explained at the beginning of each chapter. Read them carefully, so you know what skills you're expected to develop. There is more information about Outcomes and Assessment Standards at: www.sqa.org.uk/sqa/45673.html

MY NATIONAL 4 ENGLISH TARGETS

You will be asked to think about your personal goals or targets for each language skill at the beginning of each chapter. For example, in the 'Key skill – reading' chapter that follows, you are asked to think about how you are doing in reading, and what you would like to improve. Then, at the end of each chapter, you are asked to create a skill 'action plan' if there is anything you still want to improve.

THINGS TO DO AND THINK ABOUT

So what are **your** personal targets for National 4 English Course? You might want to pass National 4 English so that you can move on to National 5 English next year or because the Modern Apprenticeship you want to do asks for National 4 English. You might want to improve your writing to complete job applications. Or you might need National 4 English to get into a course at college.

Look at the table below. Some pupils have already completed it. Read their goals, then think about what your own goals are for National 4 English. Write them in the table.

Name of pupil	I want to pass National 4 English because...
Zoe	I want to attend college to do a nursery nursing course.
Sean	I want to be able to read well because I want to run my own company some day.
Lindsay	I want to work in radio so I need to speak well and be good at discussion.
Your name _____	I ...

KEY SKILL – READING

READING IN NATIONAL 4 ENGLISH

The focus in this chapter is on reading. Reading is one of the skills (or Outcomes) in the Analysis and Evaluation Unit. It is also one of the skills (or Outcomes) in the Literacy Unit. To achieve a pass in Reading (in English **and** Literacy) at National 4 level, you have to show you can read and understand written texts.

This chapter will help you to:

- understand what you read   ▪ analyse what you read   ▪ evaluate what you read.

READING: WHAT SKILLS WILL I DEVELOP?

The Outcomes and Assessment Standards for reading in the Analysis and Evaluation Unit and in the Literacy Unit are shown side-by-side in the table below.

	Analysis and Evaluation Unit	Literacy Unit
Outcomes	1. Understand, analyse and evaluate straightforward written texts by:	1. Read and understand straightforward word-based texts by:
Assessment Standards	1.1 Identifying the purpose and audience, as appropriate to genre 1.2 Identifying the main idea and supporting details 1.3 Applying knowledge of language to explain meaning and effect	1.1 Selecting and using relevant information 1.2 Explaining aspects including audience and purpose 1.3 Commenting on effectiveness

READING OUTCOMES AND ASSESSMENT STANDARDS EXPLAINED

So, to pass National 4 English, you need to show that you can do the following:

UNDERSTAND WRITTEN TEXTS

To show that you understand written texts, you need to show that you know why the text has been written (**the purpose**) and who is likely to read it (**the audience**). You also need to show that you can find the **ideas** and explain **what** the text tells you.

ANALYSE WRITTEN TEXTS

Analysing a text means commenting on the words, phrases, structures and ideas the writer has used. You need to show that you understand **how** a text has been written. For example, you may be asked to explain why a writer has used a particular word.

EVALUTE WRITTEN TEXTS

This means giving your opinion about **how well** a text has been written. For example, you might be asked about whether a writer has written clearly about a topic or whether the information is confusing.

You will develop each of these skills as you work through this chapter.

⚙ **ACTIVITY:** How am I Doing?

Before you begin, think about how you rate your reading skills and fill in the grid at the top of page 9. Be honest! **Red** means that you find the skill challenging (or that you are unsure what it means). **Amber** means that you need more practice in the skill. **Green** means that you are confident in the skill.

DON'T FORGET

The Analysis and Evaluation Unit **and** the Literacy Unit both develop your **understanding** skills.

DON'T FORGET

The Analysis and Evaluation Unit **and** the Literacy Unit both develop your **analysing** skills.

DON'T FORGET

The Analysis and Evaluation Unit **and** the Literacy Unit both develop your **evaluating** skills.

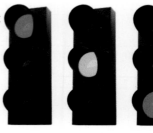

Reading skills	Red	Amber	Green
I can understand the ideas in the texts I read.			
I can analyse the texts I read.			
I can evaluate the texts I read.			

DON'T FORGET

Answer as honestly as you can! Use a tick to show how you rate yourself.

FICTION OR NON-FICTION?

Remember that in the Literacy Unit you will probably develop your reading skills by reading non-fiction, so it is important that you can recognise the difference between fiction and non-fiction. The following activity will give you some practice at doing this.

 LEARNING TOGETHER: Fiction Or Non-Fiction

TASK 1

Look at the two extracts below – one is fiction and one is non-fiction. Read them both and then look at the instructions that follow with your partner.

'Let's go somewhere else,' said Megan to her brother Bobby playing on the beach with his pail and spade. 'Let's go to the lighthouse.'...

... 'I don't want to go to the lighthouse,' he said, running over and butting her in the stomach with his head.

'But I do,' she said, skipping off lightly over the sand.

'Wait for me,' he called, picking up his pail and spade and trailing after her.

Together they walked along in a friendly way, going at a pace that suited them both. The day was warm but with a bit of wind. Megan almost felt happy. They came to a part of the shore that was deserted except for a woman walking her dog in the distance. Bobby stopped to gather shells.

Throw them away,' said Megan. 'You'll get better ones at the lighthouse.'

He emptied his pail then asked if the lighthouse was over there, pointing to the sea wall.

'Don't be stupid. The lighthouse is miles away.'

He said emphatically, 'Then I don't want to go.'

(Extract from 'The Lighthouse' in *Agnes Owens: The Complete Short Stories* by Agnes Owens, Polygon, 2008)

Horse sculptures trot in to boost visitors to Hamilton

A tourist trail of giant Clydesdale horse sculptures will be set out around Hamilton next summer in a bid to boost visitors to the South Lanarkshire town.

The 10-week "Ready Steady Gallop" event will see 30 life-sized horses, designed and painted by local artists, placed at prominent locations.

Hamilton businesses will be encouraged to sponsor a horse. At the end of the project, the sculptures will be auctioned off with proceeds going to Kilbryde Hospice.

Ready Steady Gallop is being organised by Hamilton Business Improvement District (BID) and Wild in Art, a firm which produces "mass participation art events". Gareth Walker, Hamilton BID manager, said: "This is the first event of its kind in the west of Scotland and it is going to be something really special for locals and visitors to get involved with'...

The Clydesdale was chosen as the theme for the event due to Hamilton's proximity to the Clydesdale Valley.

Organisers want to celebrate the role of the animals in the livelihoods of people who worked the land throughout Lanarkshire.

Wild in Art director Charlie Langhorne said: "We hope the industries and businesses in Hamilton will recognise the cultural benefits of sponsoring a sculpture as well as the positives for their own community.

(BBC news retrieved 25.06.14 http://www.bbc.co.uk/news/uk-scotland-glasgow-west-25087376)

TASK 2

With your partner, compare the two extracts and see how many differences and how many similarities you can find, for example, both are written in paragraphs. Now share your ideas with the rest of your group. Be prepared to share your ideas with the rest of the class, too.

 THINGS TO DO AND THINK ABOUT

Do you know your fiction from your non-fiction? Test yourself by doing the activities at www.bbc.co.uk/bitesize/ks3/english/reading/text_types/activity/.

READING DIFFERENT TEXTS

PREPARING TO READ NON-FICTION TEXTS

Prepare to read any non-fiction text by asking yourself the following questions:

WHAT DO I KNOW ALREADY?

Think about what you already know about the topic. For example, if you are reading a newspaper article with the title *Stirling Castle is Scotland's top tourist attraction* you might already know a few facts about Stirling Castle such as its history or what it looks like.

 LEARNING TOGETHER: What Do We Know?

Work with a partner to ask the question 'What do **we** know?' about the topic so you can share what you both know before you read. Look through any newspaper and pick out a headline. What do you both already know about this topic?

WHAT DO I WANT TO FIND OUT?

In the example above, you might want to find out how many people visit Stirling Castle every year, why it is the most popular attraction or what the other top Scottish tourist attractions are.

 ACTIVITY

Look at the titles below. Choose **one** of the titles.

- Formula 1 Grand Prix Shock (newspaper article)
- Exploring Disneyland (film documentary)
- Recycling in your Area (leaflet)
- Teapots of the World - all you need to know (website)
- The Causes of World War One (textbook)

Now ask yourself the following questions about your chosen title:

- What do I know already?
- What do I want to find out?

For example, you might know a lot of facts about Disneyland such as where it is and what you can do there. You might want to find out how much it costs and where you can stay. Write down your answers.

WHAT DID I LEARN?

Ask yourself this question after you have read the text. You might have learned some interesting facts or you might have learned about the writer's opinions. This depends on the type of text you are reading.

 LEARNING TOGETHER: What Did I Learn?

Choose one of the activities below after you have read any non-fiction text. First ask yourself 'What did I learn?', then work with a partner or the rest of your group to:

- make a list of things you learned and make up a quiz for the rest of the class
- create a leaflet based on ideas in the text
- think, pair and share your ideas for a board game based on the text, then make the board game
- create a poster using information from the text.

 DON'T FORGET

The introduction, any headings or list of contents and illustrations/diagrams will also help you to understand a text before you read it.

 ONLINE

Check out http://www.englishbiz.co.uk/mainguides/nonfiction.htm#ads for some more information about non-fiction, fiction (and media) texts. This is a great website with lots of helpful advice about English.

PREPARING TO READ FICTION TEXTS

You can use the same approach if you are preparing to read any fiction text. Fiction texts include novels, short stories, films, plays and poems. Again, ask yourself the following questions:

WHAT DO I KNOW ALREADY?

Think about what you already know about the book. For example, the title, the author's name and the blurb on the back of the book will give you some useful information to start with. You might know the author already (because you have read some of their other books). You might already know something about the type of book it is.

WHAT DO I WANT TO FIND OUT?

You will probably want to know what happens – for example, whether a story or film has a happy or a sad ending.

WHAT DID I LEARN?

You might have learned something about a character which made you think about yourself. You might have learned something about dealing with challenges in life. Or you might have learned about how and why people fall in love.

 **ACTIVITY**

Choose one of the activities below after you have read any fiction text. First ask yourself 'What did I learn?', then work with a partner or the rest of your group to:

- make up some interview questions you would like to ask the author/film director
- create a poster about the main character
- create a book trailer for a novel, play or film
- research any aspect of the text – for example, the setting.

GET READING!

Here are some tips to help you when you are reading:

- **Skim the text** – this means reading a text quickly to get the overall idea without reading any of the details.
- **Scan the text** – this means reading for specific information such as looking for specific ideas or numbers.
- **Look at the title and/or introduction** – does it help you to work out what the text will be about?
- **Use a highlighter as you read** – this will help you to identify key words or phrases you don't know or to highlight key ideas.

 LEARNING TOGETHER: Which Approach?

Have you tried any of the approaches above? If so, which do you find helpful when you first read a text? Write down your ideas. Now discuss with your partner why you think this approach or these approaches help you to understand a text. Be prepared to share your ideas with the rest of the class.

 THINGS TO DO AND THINK ABOUT

The best way to develop your reading skills is – obviously – to read. Get into the habit of using a dictionary for any words you come across that you don't know. That way, you will build up your vocabulary. You can then use these words in your own writing.

DON'T FORGET

If you are preparing to see a film, the trailer can give you lots of clues about it before you see it.

ONLINE

Have a look at www.scottishbooktrust.com. Type 'Book Trailer Masterclass' into the search window and you will find advice about how to create a digital book trailer with lots of great examples, too.

ONLINE

For something to read check out http://www.theguardian.com/books/teen-books for lots of reading suggestions.

UNDERSTANDING WHAT YOU READ: INTERVIEWS

The activities in this section will help you to develop your skills in understanding texts. They will help you put into practice the skills described on page 8.

You'll start by reading a non-fiction text – an interview.

THINKING ABOUT INTERVIEWS

You can watch and listen to interviews every day on radio and television. For example, a television or radio news reporter might be interviewing a politician, or a police officer might be interviewing a suspect in a television soap opera.

Remember that interviews can also be written. Written interviews often appear in magazines and newspapers. It can sometimes help you to understand an interview by reading it aloud (as if it were on radio or television or online).

LEARNING TOGETHER:
Fraser Doherty – How I Set Up SuperJam

This interview is with Fraser Doherty from Edinburgh who started a business when he was a teenager.

There are questions to check your understanding of what has been said each time Fraser is asked a question and gives his answer. You can either answer these questions as you go along or you can wait until you have read the whole interview, then answer all the questions at once. Work with a partner to answer the questions if you prefer.

Q. WHAT INSPIRED YOU TO START MAKING JAM AT THE AGE OF 14?

A. I was really excited by my gran's jam and having always enjoyed it growing up, thought that it would be fun to make some myself. I thought that if people liked it then there would be a way for me to sell it and make some extra pocket money, but that was as far as my ambitions went at that point.

Q. DID YOU THEN BEGIN TO SELL THE JAM?

A. Yes, we began selling the jam door-to-door in the area, and in some local shops and farmers' markets. People just seemed to really love the product and I started to get some press attention and I found myself on page three of the Edinburgh *Evening News* when I was 15. Other shops started calling me up about the jam and the whole thing just grew and grew. It soon got to the point where I was making hundreds of jars of jam every week in my parents' kitchen, so they were struggling to get in there to cook dinner!

DON'T FORGET

You could use the 'What do I know already?' and 'What do I want to find out?' questions before reading the interview. Remember to ask 'What have I learned?' at the end.

DON'T FORGET

Use any of the tips on page 20 to help you to understand the interview. For example, skimming is a very useful way of reading a text for the first time. Read the title, then skim quickly through the whole text so you get the overall idea of what it is about.

What inspired Fraser to start making jam?

What did Fraser hope to do by selling his jam?

Name two places where Fraser sold his jam.

Why were Fraser's parents 'struggling... to cook dinner'?

Q. WHAT WAS THE NEXT STEP?

A. It got to the stage when I couldn't go much further with the product without moving into a factory. At that point, I realised that I wanted to try to make a career out of it. I did some research and found that sales of jam had been in decline for the past couple of decades. This was partly because jam is traditionally very unhealthy and has an old-fashioned image. I figured if I could create a healthier and modern brand of jam, then maybe I could challenge the trend of declining sales. I came up with a way of making jam completely from fruit juice, not using anything artificial or adding any sugar. Then I decided that I was going to try to sell the product to the big supermarkets.

> What did Fraser's research tell him about sales of jam?
>
> What two things did Fraser do to make his jam healthier than other jams?

Q. WHAT DID YOU DO THEN AND HOW DID YOU FUND IT?

A. I spent a couple of years convincing a factory and an advertising agency to work with me. I eventually got production up and running: we moved into the factory in 2006 and created the brand that we have now. I had a little bit of money that I had saved myself and got a loan from the Prince's Trust for £5000.

> How did Fraser fund his jam-making business?

Q. DID ALL THIS WORK PAY OFF?

A. One supermarket agreed to try it out in their stores in March 2007. On the first day in one of the Edinburgh stores they sold 1500 jars, which was more jam than they would normally sell in a month. They had never seen anything like it. Then another supermarket phoned up out of the blue and said that they would like to stock it, then another; now all of the major retailers stock SuperJam.

> Why was it surprising that the first supermarket sold 1500 jars on the first day?

Q. WHAT ADVICE WOULD YOU GIVE ABOUT RUNNING A BUSINESS?

A. Go out and give things a shot. Don't be afraid to try things and see what you learn. On a practical level, the best help that I've had has been from mentors. Entrepreneurs should look to anyone that has run a business or a charity, someone who has been there and done it, and can provide you with a great opportunity to learn.

> What two pieces of advice does Fraser give about running a business?
>
> Why does Fraser think a mentor is a good idea?

(Interview adapted from http://www.newbusiness.co.uk/articles/entrepreneurs/fraser-doherty-how-i-set-superjam)

THINGS TO DO AND THINK ABOUT

Did you understand the interview? Were there words and phrases you didn't understand? Work with your partner and share any words or phrases or sections you were not sure of. Help each other to work out the meaning – use a dictionary if you need one. Now share your ideas with the rest of your group/class.

UNDERSTANDING WHAT YOU READ: AUDIENCE AND PURPOSE

In the next few activities, you are going to focus on who is going to read the text (**audience**) and why the text has been written (**purpose**). You need to be able to identify audience and purpose no matter what text you are reading.

WORKING OUT THE AUDIENCE AND PURPOSE

To work out the audience and purpose of a text, think about the

- language
- format
- style
- ideas.

AUDIENCE

Who is the text aimed at? Think about being in the audience when you are watching a film at the cinema or watching a band play at a music festival. When you read a text, you are the 'audience' for that text.

 LEARNING TOGETHER: Who Is The Audience?

TASK 1

Look at the headlines of the newspaper articles below. Which one sounds most interesting to you?

Discuss with your partner which headline you chose and why. Be prepared to share your ideas with the rest of the group/class.

You might have chosen 'Teenager wins celebrity lookalike contest' because you are a teenager and/or because you are interested in celebrities – so **you** are the target audience for this article!

Of course, you might have chosen 'Prime Minister opens Highland railway line' if you live in the Highlands or you might have chosen 'African government aims to boost employment' if you are doing an International Issues topic in Modern Studies about Africa.

Prime Minister opens Highland railway line

'African government aims to boost employment'

Teenager wins celebrity lookalike contest

TASK 2

To work out who might read a text, think about who the text is aimed at.

Text	Features	Audience example	Language example
Short story	-Very simple language -Very large font -Short sentences -Bright pictures	Young child	'The big bad wolf smiled.'
Scientific report	-Complex language -Complex ideas -Long sentences -Statistics -Diagrams	Scientist or science student	'To identify this type of DNA, proteins are purified from cell extracts of cultures which have been grown for at least three months.'
Advertisement for supermarket	-Persuasive language -Short sentences -Friendly tone -Bright pictures	Potential customers	'Excellence. Simply Delivered.'

DON'T FORGET

Sometimes texts are written for the general public – for example, a leaflet sent by the government to every household in Scotland or a BBC online news article.

TASK 3

Try re-writing a text for different audiences. You can have great fun doing this!

Sort yourself into three pairs. Each pair has to write a slightly different recipe for a chocolate cake (or a dish of your choice). First, find any recipe, for example from a website or cookery book.

- One pair writes the recipe for a very young child to read.
- One pair writes the recipe for a teenager who has never baked a cake before.
- One pair writes the recipe for an expert adult baker.

Now share with the group how you and your partner changed the language, format, layout, style and ideas for each different reader or 'audience'. Be prepared to share your ideas with the rest of the class.

PURPOSE

What is the text for? Think about why a text has been written or created. Here are some examples:

Example of text	Purpose
-DIY leaflet -Recipe	To instruct
-Letter from council -Healthy eating leaflet	To instruct
-TV documentary -School textbook	To inform
-Advertisement -Healthy eating leaflet	To persuade
-Novel -TV comedy -YouTube clip	To entertain
-Travel brochure	To describe
-Poem	To entertain
-Film review -Travel website	To review

 ONLINE

Watch the film clip at http://www.bbc.co.uk/learningzone/clips/adapting-writing-for-different-purposes/743.html which is about turning one type of writing into another. Try this for yourself by writing about a trip or journey or holiday you have taken. Then turn this writing into a piece that is useful for tourists – the purposes will be to inform and to instruct.

 DON'T FORGET

Texts can have more than one purpose. A party invitation might include directions to **explain** how to get to the venue, **inform** you of the date and time and **persuade** you to attend the party! The important thing is to be able to identify the **main** purpose. (The main purpose of a party invitation is to invite you to the party!)

 ACTIVITY: Fraser Doherty's Website

Fraser Doherty has his own website at http://www.fraserdoherty.com. Browse carefully through the website. What do you think its purpose is, and which audience is Fraser trying to reach?

"FROM MY GRAN'S KITCHEN TO THE SUPERMARKET SHELVES AND BEYOND."

 THINGS TO DO AND THINK ABOUT

Choose an activity from the list below:

- Create a mind map of all Fraser's SuperJam products including types of jam, honey and books.
- Write a biography of Fraser Doherty's life.
- Give a talk about Fraser Doherty and how he started his business.
- Write some interview questions to ask Fraser Doherty.
- Write a letter to Fraser asking him to your school to give a talk.
- Create a poster about Fraser Doherty using images and words.

ANALYSING WHAT YOU READ: ADVERTISEMENTS

The activities in this section will help you to develop your skills in **analysing** texts.

First, you will analyse an advertisement to understand the techniques that advertisers use to grab the reader's attention. Then you will create an advertisement for one of Fraser's SuperJam products.

⚙ ACTIVITY: Analysing An Advertisement 1

First, have a look at this advertisement for a restaurant on the island of Arran. With a partner, discuss the advertisement and answer the questions below:

- Who is the advertisement aimed at? Give your reasons.
- What are the key messages in the advertisement?
- What overall impression do you get about the restaurant?
- What do you like/dislike about the advertisement?
- How successful is the advertisement in encouraging you to visit this restaurant?

DON'T FORGET

Remember that analysing a text means looking at **how** a text has been written. Look back at the introduction to this chapter for more information about analysing texts.

Don't visit Arran

without sampling the delights of Brodick's new seafront restaurant, **Arran on a Plate**

Here you can enjoy seasonal local produce at affordable prices, prepared by Arran's only Master Chef of Great Britain.

As you might expect, tantalising seafood is always on the menu, which changes daily. Meat eaters and vegetarians will also find plenty to tickle their taste buds: exotic wild mushroom risotto, Lochranza venison in chocolate sauce and surprising soufflés are to be discovered among the daily delights.

Dinner typically begins with a complimentary pre-starter and concludes with a hand-made sweetmeat. Altogether a memorable experience, at a bargain price.

It's advisable to book a table as this eatery is already turning away customers at busy periods due to its popularity.

OPEN SEVEN DAYS A WEEK

Cocktail bar licensed until midnight

Arran ON A PLATE

Lunch
2-Courses £10 • 3-Courses £15
served from 12 noon — last orders 2.30pm

Dinner
2-Courses £20 • 3-Courses £25
served from 5.30pm — last orders 9.30pm

Booking recommmended but not essential

Telephone: 01770 303 886
E-mail: bookings@arranonaplate.com
www.arranonaplate.com

LANGUAGE TECHNIQUES

Eight techniques often used in advertisements are shown in the table – Ewan has added some examples and explanations of why he thinks these techniques are effective.

Technique	Explanation	Advertised product	Ewan's examples	Ewan's explanations
Alliteration	Repeating sounds at the beginnings of words/ phrases	Marmalade	Tempting and tasty on toast!	The writer has used alliteration to... create a catchy phrase the reader will remember

Adjectives	Words and phrases used to describe a product	Holiday	Stunning scenery	The writer has used an adjective to... help the reader to visualise the landscape
Punctuation	Using punctuation for effect	Sports car	THE car company!	The writer has used capital letters and underlining to... emphasise that this car company is the only one that can provide what the reader needs
Repetition	Repeating words or phrases	Chocolate biscuit	Yum, yum	The writer has used repetition to... emphasise the idea that the biscuit is very tasty
Rhetorical question	A question which makes the reader think about his/her response	Yoghurt	Do you want to eat more healthily?	The writer has used a rhetorical question to... make the reader think about whether he/she could eat more healthily
'rule of three'	Using three words or ideas or numbers	Shoes	Simple, supportive and stylish	The writer has used the 'rule of three' to... emphasise the three most important facts about the product
Using data	Using statistics, numbers and/or scientific information	Headphones	1 million headsets sold every week!	The writer has used statistics to... emphasise how popular the product is
Strap line	A short catchy phrase	Toothpaste	Made for smiling	The writer has used a strap line to... make the product memorable

 LEARNING TOGETHER: Spot The Technique

Try this activity with your partner. Read the advertisement for 'Arran on a Plate' again. Can you find the techniques below and explain why they have been used?

 **DON'T FORGET**

Remember that an advertisement always tries to persuade you to buy a product or influence your views/opinions about something.

Technique	Examples from 'Arran on a Plate' advertisement
Alliteration	
Adjectives	
'rule of three'	

 **ACTIVITY:** Analysing An Advertisement 2

The writer of this advertisement chose **not** to use the techniques below. With your partner, suggest some phrases/sentences/questions to add to the advertisement, using these techniques.

Technique	Ideas to add to 'Arran on a Plate' advertisement
Punctuation	
Repetition	
Rhetorical question	'Why not visit us this weekend?'
Using data	
Strap line	

 **ACTIVITY:** Creating An Advertisement

One of the best ways to learn about a technique is to use it yourself, so you are now going to create an advertisement for Fraser's SuperJam.

Read Fraser's website again to get ideas you might want to use in your advertisement.

 **ACTIVITY:** Review

In your group, take three minutes to review what you have learned so far about advertising techniques. Be prepared to share your ideas with the rest of the class.

 THINGS TO DO AND THINK ABOUT

Keep a look out for any advertisements you come across (on the bus, in the cinema, in magazines and newspapers, and in the margins of web pages) and try to identify examples of any of these language techniques. Why not try this out on the way home today?

ANALYSING WHAT YOU READ: FICTION

You have read an interview and some web pages and you have analysed an advertisement. These are all non-fiction texts. Now it is time for some fiction!

FEATURES OF FICTION

Any novel or short story usually has the following features:

- A **plot** (sometimes called a 'narrative') which is what happens in the story.
- A **setting** (where and when the story takes place).
- One or two **main characters** (and some minor, less important characters, too).
- A **main idea** or **theme**.
- A **narrator** (or the person/people telling the story) – this can be in the first person ('I') or in the third person ('he', 'she' or 'it').
- Interesting, imaginative **language**.

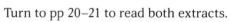

LEARNING TOGETHER: Reading Fiction

In this activity, you will read the openings of two novels which have the same theme. Both novels are about being different. *Wonder* by R J Palacio is about August, a boy who has a deformed face and who has to cope with the challenge of looking different. *Freak the Mighty* by Rodman Philbrick is about a friendship between two boys, Max and Kevin, who are 'outsiders'. When they are together, they feel more able to cope with life.

Turn to pp 20–21 to read both extracts.

Do Task 1 on your own before you share your ideas with your partner. Do Task 2 in the same way.

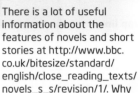

ONLINE

There is a lot of useful information about the features of novels and short stories at http://www.bbc.co.uk/bitesize/standard/english/close_reading_texts/novels_s_s/revision/1/. Why don't you watch and listen to some of the resources at this web address?

DON'T FORGET

Writers create believable characters by telling us what the characters say, think and do. Focus on what August and Max say, think and do in these openings.

TASK 1: WONDER

In your own words, explain what each paragraph is about and/or what happens in each paragraph. An example has been done for you below.

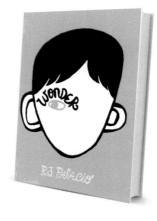

Paragraph	What is the paragraph about and/or what happens in the paragraph?
1	The paragraph is about August feeling ordinary and how people treat him. He describes ordinary things he does like playing XBox. He says other people stare at him or run away from him.
2	
3	
4	
5	
6	
7	

TASK 2: FREAK THE MIGHTY

Look at the information below. Read the text again and work out which statements are true and which are false. One has been done for you as an example.

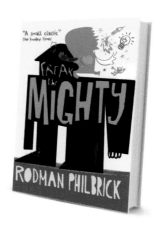

Statement	True or False?
Max feels alone until he meets Freak.	
Max often kicked people who tried to care for him.	
Max's grandparents thought he should play with children of the same age.	
Max met Freak every day in school.	False
Freak hit another pupil once.	
Freak pretended to be a robot in the playground.	
Nobody else apart from Freak called Max 'Kicker'.	

THINGS TO DO AND THINK ABOUT

Have a look at R J Palacio's website at http://rjpalacio.com/ where you can watch a video version of the opening of *Wonder*, and learn more about the novel.

ANALYSING WHAT YOU READ: NOVEL OPENINGS

SOME TIPS TO START!

Here are five top tips to help you understand what you are reading:

- Read the text through once completely. Now read it again, this time skimming through it for general ideas. Finally, read it one more time, this time scanning it for specific ideas, information or numbers.
- Look for titles, headings, sub-headings, and topic sentences – these will all help you to understand what the text is about.
- Look at how the text is laid out – is it in paragraphs, sections or columns?
- Read carefully, then look up from the text and ask yourself: 'Have I understood what I have just read?' Check back if you are not sure.
- Read right to the end. Even if you find a text difficult, keep going and don't give up!

Wonder

I know I'm not an ordinary ten-year-old kid. I mean, sure, I do ordinary things. I eat ice cream. I ride my bike. I play ball. I have an XBox. Stuff like that makes me ordinary. I guess. And I feel ordinary. Inside. But I know ordinary kids don't make other ordinary kids run away screaming in playgrounds. I know ordinary kids don't get stared at wherever they go.

If I found a magic lamp and I could have one wish, I would wish that I had a normal face that no one ever noticed at all. I would wish that I could walk down the street without people seeing me and then doing that look-away thing. Here's what I think: the only reason I'm not ordinary is that no one else sees me that way. But I'm kind of used to how I look by now. I know how to pretend I don't see the faces people make. We've all gotten pretty good at that sort of thing: me, Mom and Dad, Via. Actually, I take that back: Via's not so good at it. She can get really annoyed when people do something rude. Like, for instance, one time in the playground some older kids made some noises. I don't even know what the noises were exactly because I didn't hear them myself, but Via heard and she just started yelling at the kids. That's the way she is. I'm not that way.

Via doesn't see me as ordinary. She says she does, but if I were ordinary, she wouldn't feel like she needs to protect me as much. And Mom and Dad don't see me as ordinary, either. They see me as extraordinary. I think the only person in the world who realizes how ordinary I am is me.

My name is August, by the way. I won't describe what I look like. Whatever you're thinking, it's probably worse. Next week I start fifth grade. Since I've never been to a real school before, I am pretty much totally and completely petrified. People think I haven't gone to school because of the way I look, but it's not that. It's because of all the surgeries I've had. Twenty-seven since I was born. The bigger ones happened before I was even four years old, so I don't remember those. But I've had two or three surgeries every year since then (some big, some small), and because I'm little for my age, and I have some other medical mysteries that doctors never really figured out, I used to get sick a lot. That's why my parents decided it was better if I didn't go to school. I'm much stronger now, though. The last surgery I had was eight months ago, and I probably won't have to have any more for another couple of years.

Mom homeschools me. She used to be a children's-book illustrator. She draws really great fairies and mermaids. Her boy stuff isn't so hot, though. She once tried to draw me a Darth Vader, but it ended up looking like some weird mushroom-shaped robot. I haven't seen her draw anything in a long time. I think she's too busy taking care of me and Via.

I can't say I always wanted to go to school because that wouldn't be exactly true. What I wanted was to go to school, but only if I could be like every other kid going to school. Have lots of friends and hang out after school and stuff like that.

Freak the Mighty

I never had a brain until Freak came along and let me borrow his for a while, and that's the truth, the whole truth. The unvanquished truth, is how Freak would say it, and for a long time it was him who did the talking. Except I had a way of saying things with my fists and my feet even before we became Freak the Mighty, slaying dragons and fools and walking high above the world.

Called me Kicker for a time – this was day care, the year Gram and Grim took me over – and I had a thing about booting anyone who dared to touch me. Because they were always trying to throw a hug on me, like it was a medicine I needed.

Gram and Grim, bless their pointed little heads, they're my mother's people, her parents, and they figured whoa! better put this little critter with other little critters his own age, maybe it will improve his temper.

Yeah, right! Instead, what happened, I invented games like kick-boxing and kick-knees and kick-faces and kick-teachers, and kick-the-other-little-day-care-critters, because I knew what a rotten lie that hug stuff was. Oh, I knew.

That's when I got my first look at Freak, that year of the phoney hugs. He didn't look so different back then, we were all of us pretty small, right? But he wasn't in the playroom with us every day, just now and then he'd show up. Looking sort of fierce is how I remember him. Except later it was Freak himself who taught me that remembering is a great invention of the mind, and if you try hard enough you can remember anything, whether it really happened or not.

So maybe he wasn't really all that fierce in day care, except I'm pretty sure he did hit a kid with his crutch once, whacked the little brat pretty good. And for some reason little Kicker never got around to kicking little Freak.

Maybe it was those crutches kept me from lashing out at him, man those crutches were cool. I wanted a pair for myself. And when little Freak showed up one day with these shiny braces strapped to his crooked legs, metal tubes right up to his hips, why those were even more cool than crutches.

'I'm Robot Man,' little Freak would go, making these weird robot noises as he humped himself around the playground. Rrrr. . .rrr. . .rrr. . .like he had robot motors inside his legs, going rrrrr. . .rrrr . . .rrrr, and this look, like don't mess with me, man, maybe I got a laser cannon hidden inside these leg braces, smoke a hole right through you. No question, Freak was hooked on robots even back then, this little guy two feet tall, and already he knew what he wanted.

Then for a long time I never saw Freak any more, one day he just never came back to day care, and the next thing I remember I'm like in the third grade or something and I catch a glimpse of this yellow-haired kid scowling at me from one of those cripple vans. Man, they were death-ray eyes, and I think, hey, that's him, the robot boy, and it was like whoa! because I'd forgotten all about him, day care was a blank place in my head, and nobody had called me Kicker for a long time.

THINGS TO DO AND THINK ABOUT

Based on the opening pages, which of these novels would you like to read? Which do you prefer and why? Get together with a partner and discuss your choice.

DON'T FORGET

Ask questions such as 'What's really going on?' and 'How does he actually feel about what has happened?' to help you look for clues and understand the characters.

ANALYSING WHAT YOU READ: WRITER'S STYLE

We are going to look at three aspects of style used in *Wonder* and *Freak the Mighty*:

- who is telling the story?
- word choice
- tense

WHO IS TELLING THE STORY?

These novels are both written in the first person. This means that the main character tells the story, using 'I', 'me' and 'my'. The main character telling the story is called the narrator. Writers choose to write a story in the first person so that:

- the narrator's thoughts and feelings are spoken directly to you, the reader
- you get to know the narrator very well because everything that happens is described by him/her
- you are given only the narrator's point of view.

Writing in the third person means that the writer uses 'he/she' and 'him/her' or sometimes 'it'. Writers choose to write a story in the third person so that:

- the writer can describe the thoughts and feelings of all the characters
- you get to know all the characters very well
- you are given the points of view of all the characters.

LEARNING TOGETHER: First Or Third Person?

With your partner, discuss whether you prefer stories told in the first person or in the third person and why. Now share your ideas with the rest of the group/class.

WORD CHOICE

Think about writing an email or a postcard to a friend. You choose every word that you write in that email or postcard. All writers make choices about words.

Watch and listen to Fatimah Kelleher – a poet – explaining why she chooses particular words in her writing at http://www.bbc.co.uk/education/clips/zq7vr82

Now think about this sentence from the *Wonder* extract:

'*Since I've never been to a real school before, I am pretty much totally and completely petrified.*'

Why do you think the writer chose 'petrified' and not 'frightened' or 'scared'? Perhaps because this word means being so scared that you cannot move? This is, in fact, exactly the idea the writer wants to get across.

Think about the phrase '*whacked the little brat*' from the *Freak the Mighty* extract. Why do you think the writer used 'whacked' here and not 'hit' or 'punched'? Perhaps because the word 'whack' means to hit noisily and also because 'whack' is an example of onomatopoeia so we can imagine the sound of the hit.

TENSE

Although these openings are very similar, *Wonder* is written in the present tense (as though the events are happening now) and *Freak the Mighty* is written in the past tense (where the narrator is explaining what happened in the past).

- Writers use the present tense as if the events in the story are happening now, right in front of us.
- Writers use the past tense so that their characters can be reflective – they are remembering or retelling thoughts, feelings and events which happened in the past.

 LEARNING TOGETHER: Tenses

Read each extract again. Work with your partner to find **five** examples of sentences/phrases that are written in the **past tense** and **five** examples of sentences/phrases that are written in the **present tense**. Number 1 has been done for you. Notice that the verb has been underlined – the verb will tell if it's past tense or present tense.

	Wonder	*Freak the Mighty*
1	I <u>do</u> ordinary things.	... I <u>invented</u> games ...
2		
3		
4		
5		
6		

Discuss in your group whether you prefer novels and stories written in the present tense or in the past tense, and why.

Now give yourselves a number – 1, 2, 3 or 4. Each corner of the room has a poster with one of these numbers on it, and each corner/poster has a task:

Corner 1 – write quotations in the present tense from *Wonder*

Corner 2 – write the advantages of writing in the present tense

Corner 3 – write quotations in the past tense from *Wonder*

Corner 4 – write the advantages of writing in the past tense

When the teacher calls your number, go to the appropriate corner of the room and write down your ideas on the poster. For example, if you are number 2 in your group, you will go to corner 2 to write down an advantage of writing in the present tense.

 ## THINGS TO DO AND THINK ABOUT

Have you ever written a story where you started off in the present tense and changed to past tense halfway through? Next time you write a story, plan to use either present or past tense and stick to that throughout!

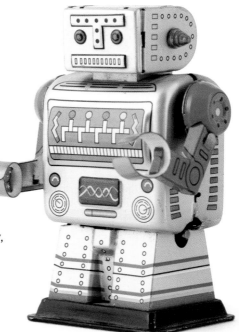

ANALYSING WHAT YOU READ: POETRY 1

You are now going to read and analyse a different type of text – a poem.

You will probably already be familiar with poetry and how this is different from other types of text. Many poems do not follow the usual rules about capital letters, full stops and all the other punctuation you have to remember when writing sentences. Poetry is really about 'playing with' words, phrases and ideas.

POETRY TECHNIQUES

When you are analysing a poem, it is important that you know the techniques poets use to create poems. Have a look below at some poetry techniques.

Technique	Explanation	Example
Alliteration	Repetition of sounds at the beginning of words	*Beautiful bouncing ball*
Assonance	Repetition of vowel sounds within words	*How now brown cow*
End rhyme	Rhyming words at the end of lines	*Humpty Dumpty sat on a wall, Humpty Dumpty had a great fall*
Imagery	Language used to create images in the reader's mind	*The juicy tomato burst in her mouth*
Internal rhyme	Use of rhyming words within a line	*Double, double toil and trouble, Fire burn and cauldron bubble*
Onomatopoeia	Words which sound very much like the noise they name	*Splash!*
Simile	A comparison of two things using 'like' or 'as'	*Hair like gold*
Metaphor	A comparison of two things that are very different, but have certain things in common	*Ice cold stare*
Personification	Describing an object as if it were a person	*The fire raged*
Repetition	Repeating a word or phrase	*Believe in yourself and you will go far. Believe in yourself. Believe in yourself and the sky's the limit.*
Rhythm	The pattern of sounds created by syllables in a line/verse	*I wandered, lonely as a cloud…*

ONLINE

Have you read any poems by EE Cummings? He does not use any punctuation at all in his poems! Have a look at *anyone lived in a pretty how town* at http://www.poets.org/poetsorg/poem/anyone-lived-pretty-how-town

LEARNING TOGETHER:
Analysing A Poem

TASK 1

Before you read the poem below, discuss Indian restaurants you have visited and/or any types of Indian food you know about with your partner. Share your ideas with the rest of the group/class.

TASK 2

Now, read the poem *Guid Taste*. The poet is anonymous.

TASK 3

Guid Taste

Tae get your juices gaun we've

the brawest Indian food fur ye.

Goan specialities

caller oot o Scotland's seas.

King prawns hottered wi a sauce,

tomatay, ingan, special spice;

a yoghurt pickle mixter-maxter,

rice maskit wi fine rose watter.

Try Shabnam, a receipt fae

the fithills o the Himalayas;

a wee paratha oan the side,

Basmati birled wi mustard seed.

A toothsome dish wi plenty teeth,

oor het an sherp Jalfrezie

isnae fur the chucken hertit!

– jist fur fowk that like it gey het.

(Scottish anonymous)

(http://www.Scottishpoetrylibrary.org.uk/
poetry/poems/guid-taste)

Make sure that you understand all the words in the poem before you analyse it. For example, the poet mentions typical Indian ingredients or dishes:

- king prawns
- tomatay (tomato)
- ingan (onion)
- spice
- yoghurt pickle
- rice
- rose watter (rose water)
- paratha
- basmati
- mustard seed

If you aren't sure what some of these ingredients or dishes are, do some research to find out.

TASK 4

Look at the questions below and discuss your answers with a partner.

- What is the main idea or message in the poem?
- Who would enjoy reading this poem?
- What is the poet's purpose in writing this poem?
- What interesting or effective words has the poet chosen? Highlight words you find interesting or effective and discuss your reasons.
- What is the structure or shape of the poem? (Does the poem rhyme? How many verses and lines does it have?)
- What is the tone or 'feeling' of the poem? (Sad, happy, intense, thoughtful?) Underline any words or phrases that create this tone.

TASK 5

Read the poem again with your partner, then discuss and answer these questions:

- Have you tried any or all of the ingredients above? Did you know what they are? (Use a dictionary/do an internet search if you need to.)
- Look at the phrases 'Tae get your juices gaun', 'the brawest Indian food', 'specialities', 'a toothsome dish'. What is the poet saying about Indian food by using these descriptions?
- What is the poet saying about Indian food and how it is made?
- What is the poem's message about Indian food in Scotland?

TASK 6

When you have shared your ideas, discuss them with your group. Your group could create a poster for the poem – perhaps you could place the poem in the centre of the poster and illustrate it/place your ideas around it?

THINGS TO DO AND THINK ABOUT

Look at http://www.dsl.ac.uk/ - this is a Scots dictionary where you can find definitions of Scottish words. Use it to look up some words from the poem and/or any Scots words you know/use. For example, 'scunner', 'glaikit', 'ken' and so on.

ANALYSING WHAT YOU READ: POETRY 2

TALKING ABOUT WORD PLAY

There are several phrases in the poem with a 'double meaning'. This is sometimes called 'word play'. For example, someone with good taste is someone who is good at judging what is beautiful or pleasing, such as a beautiful building. 'Good taste' also means, obviously, something which tastes good and the poem is all about delicious Indian food!

Another example of word play is 'a toothsome dish wi' plenty teeth'. 'Toothsome' means 'tasty' and 'wi plenty teeth' is an image. There are no actual teeth in the dish! This means that the dish is sharp and spicy.

A final example – the dish is not for the 'chucken hertit' which means cowardly. A Jalfrezie dish often contains chicken, which is another reason the poet has chosen the phrase 'chucken hertit'.

 LEARNING TOGETHER: Talking About Scots

TASK 1

Why do you think the poet has used word play in this way? Discuss with your partner then share your ideas with the rest of the group/class.

TASK 2

Here is the poem written in Standard English, beside the original version. Which version do you think is better, and why?

Guid Taste	Good Taste
Tae get your juices gaun we've	To get your juices flowing we've
the brawest Indian food fur ye.	the best Indian food for you.
Goan specialities	Goan specialities
caller oot o Scotland's seas.	fresh out of Scotland's seas.
King prawns hottered wi a sauce,	King prawns boiled up with a sauce,
tomatay, ingan, special spice;	tomato, onion, special spice;
a yoghurt pickle mixter-maxter,	a yoghurt pickle all jumbled up,
rice maskit wi fine rose watter.	rice covered with fine rose water.
Try Shabnam, a receipt fae	Try Shabnam, a recipe from
the fithills o the Himalayas;	the foothills of the Himalayas;
a wee paratha oan the side,	a small paratha on the side,
Basmati birled wi mustard seed.	Basmati stirred round with mustard seed.
A toothsome dish wi plenty teeth,	A tasty dish with plenty of teeth,
oor het an sherp Jalfrezie	our hot and sharp Jalfrezie
isnae fur the chucken hertit!	isn't for the chicken-hearted!
- jist fur fowk that like it gey het.	– just for people that like it really hot.

 ONLINE

Watch and listen to the clip at http://www.bbc.co.uk/education/clips/zm23cdm where Sanjeev Kholi talks about the Scots language – and uses some great Scottish insults!

TASK 3

How many Scots words did you know in the poem? There are many examples, including 'brawest', 'birled' and 'fowk'. Looking at the Standard English version if you need to, underline all the Scots words in the original version. Why do you think the poet has chosen to write the poem using Scots words and phrases? Discuss this with your partner, then share your ideas with the group/class.

TONE AND ATTITUDE

The **tone** of this poem is humorous and light-hearted. Some of the humour in the poem comes from unusual words or ideas being placed beside each other. For example, a 'receipt' is a very old Scots word for 'recipe'. This word is placed before the phrase 'fae the fithills o the Himalayas' to create a humorous effect. Another example is the use of 'basmati' alongside 'birled' – two words that are not often placed together!

The tone of a text can help you to work out the writer's **attitude** (their opinions and feelings about the topic or theme of the text). Here, the writer uses a light-hearted tone and humour to show his attitude that Indian food is something to be enjoyed!

 LEARNING TOGETHER: Examples Of Humour

Work with a partner to find as many examples of light-hearted tone or humour in the poem as you can.

 ACTIVITY: Review

Take three minutes in your group to review what you have learned so far about poetry techniques. Be prepared to share your ideas with the rest of the group/class.

THINGS TO DO AND THINK ABOUT

Carry out some research on one aspect of the poem. For example, you could find out about some of the ingredients mentioned, or you could research an aspect of the Scots language at www.scotslanguage.com, where you can hear different words and phrases used in different parts of Scotland.

ANALYSING WHAT YOU READ: ONLINE NEWS

It's time to return to non-fiction with a news article from *The Daily What* at www.dailywhat.org.uk

But first, think about what you normally see in newspaper articles.

 LEARNING TOGETHER: Analysing Online News

TASK 1

Create a newspaper graffiti board. (A graffiti board is where you can place lots of ideas on one topic – it's a type of poster.)

Each member of the group should bring in a print newspaper. Try to ensure that you have a variety of papers. Share these with the group. What have you found out about:

- how newspapers are laid out?
- what news stories are covered?
- what kind of language is used?

You could find examples (such as headlines) to stick onto your graffiti board. Your graffiti board could even be designed to look like a newspaper front page!

TASK 2

Now read the news article below:

> **DON'T FORGET** +
>
> Print news articles are usually written in columns. Online news articles are sometimes written in columns but can be laid out differently – for example, in paragraphs. News articles are usually written in short paragraphs and the language is clear and factual. There are usually photographs with captions, too.

LARRY AND THE DOWNING STREET CATS

David Cameron's Chief Mouser of 10 Downing Street is a tabby named Larry, a rescue cat from Battersea Dogs and Cats Home – a choice made by the Prime Minister's children.

Three years ago, the cat was found wandering the streets of London and was taken in to the rescue centre. Within a month, he became Britain's most famous kitty.

The Prime Minister has thanked the home by saying "I'm delighted to welcome Larry to his new home. He came highly recommended to me by Battersea Dogs and Cats Home, who did a fantastic job looking after him. I'm sure he will be a great addition to Downing Street and will charm our many visitors." Thanks to Larry's publicity, the rescue centre has seen a 15% rise in cat adoptions.

Larry is the latest in the line of Number 10 cats. Those cats that sauntered before him include Sybil, Gordon Brown's kitty, and 10 years before her, Humphrey who ended his service in 1997.

Larry made his first public killing on August 28 2012, proudly displaying the body of a mouse on the front garden of 10 Downing Street – flaunting his skill to the press. According to Larry's official Downing Street webpage, "Larry spends his days greeting guests to the house, inspecting security defences and testing

Larry meets Barrack Obama.

antique furniture for napping quality. His day-to-day responsibilities also include contemplating a solution to the mouse occupancy of the house. Larry says this is still 'in tactical planning stage'."

Now Larry shares his street with neighbour George Osborne's cat Freya, appointed in 2012. Although the two tabbies have engaged in a fight with each other, they do continue to share their position. However, when asked about their relationship, a Number 10 spokesperson simply said "they co-exist".

Despite the rumours of his retirement, and his less than friendly gestures towards some reporters in the past, Larry remains 'top dog' at 10 Downing Street. He has many dedicated fans across the globe and several websites, including several mock Twitter accounts.

(Article from https://www.dailywhat.org.uk/2014/01/cats-may-get-jobs-in-westminster.aspx)

LEARNING TOGETHER: *Of Mice And Men*

TASK 1

You will work on this extract with your partner. First, read the extract again and make sure you understand it all. Look up any words you don't know. Discuss the opening with your partner – does he/she understand everything?

TASK 2

The novel begins with a description of a riverbank surrounded by trees. With your partner, highlight or underline three phrases in the first two paragraphs that make the setting sound **pleasant** and **inviting**. Next, highlight or underline three phrases in the first two paragraphs that you think make the setting sound **calm** and **peaceful**. Write these phrases in the table below. One is done for you.

Pleasant and inviting setting	Calm and peaceful setting
1 "The water is warm"	1
2	2
3	3

TASK 3

Now complete the table below to show the differences between George and Lennie. One has been done for you. Refer to paragraph 4 to find the answers.

	George	Lennie
Clothing		
Possessions		
Size	"small"	"huge"
Face		
Hands		
Arms		
Any other differences		

TASK 4

You are now going to evaluate this extract. With your partner, discuss the following questions, tick the evaluation you agree with and then give a reason for this evaluation in the last column.

Question	Your evaluation (please tick)	Reason(s) for your evaluation
How effective is the description of Lennie?	Very effective ☐ Effective ☐ Not effective ☐	
How effective is the description of the setting?	Very effective ☐ Effective ☐ Not effective ☐	
How effective is the opening in making you want to read on and find out what happens?	Very effective ☐ Effective ☐ Not effective ☐	

Now share your evaluations with the rest of your group. Be ready to give reasons for your opinions.

 ONLINE

Pinterest (www.pinterest.com) is a website where you can create and share images. You could create a pinterest board with images of *Of Mice and Men* – or any other novel you have read and enjoyed.

 THINGS TO DO AND THINK ABOUT

John Steinbeck wants to show that George is like a parent to Lennie. Discuss how successful John Steinbeck is in showing that George and Lennie have a parent/child relationship.

READING ASSESSMENT

Try this assessment to test your reading skills.

 ACTIVITY: Test Your Reading Skills

First, read this article from the online newspaper 'The Daily What'.

BRANDING MATTERS

Some notable brands and rebrands by Kathryn Carberry, Clydeview Academy.

Fail: Edinburgh City Council
"Incredinburgh" was a £300000 marketing campaign designed to promote Edinburgh in 2012. It was condemned by a senior councillor and generated widespread negative reactions. Despite the investment it was never actually used.

Fail: Royal Mail
Some bright spark had the idea of renaming Her Majesty's mail service Consignia as part of a £2million rebrand. Apparently, the name was chosen as a mix of the words 'consign' and 'insignia', and was seen as symbolizing trustworthiness – although one member of the public pointed out that Consignia Plc is actually an anagram of Panic Closing. Following the backlash Consignia was binned in 2002 and the company was named Royal Mail which included Post Office. Simples.

Fail: Newcastle United FC
In October 2011 Newcastle United rebranded their famous St James' Park Stadium as the Sports Direct Stadium. It made no difference to the fans who continued to refer to it as St James' Park. A year later they removed the branding.

Hmm: Starbucks
Who could have thought that a sliding Starbucks van door would turn their brand name into a word "Sucks" right next to the logo? What a fail! But the brand seems to have weathered the internet photo storm.

Hmm: Snickers
People still like to talk about Marathons which became Snickers in 1990. There were rumours in 2008 that the brand would go back to its original UK name as Mars re-registered the name.

Win: Pepsi
Pepsi was developed in 1893 and introduced as Brad's Drink. It was renamed as Pepsi-Cola on August 28, 1898. Much more fizz!

Win: Google
Google started out as a project called BackRub. That might not have been quite right for a multinational company. Most people don't have a clue what the word google means. But they know what Google is! It is now even a verb. And if you don't believe me, just google it!

(Adapted from www.dailywhat.org.uk/2014/01/branding-matters.aspx)

Now answer the questions below on your own.

1. What is the main purpose of this news article? Why do you think this is the main purpose?

2. Who would enjoy reading this news article?

Audience	Yes/no	Why/why not?
Consumers of the products mentioned		
Manufacturers of the products mentioned		

3. Explain the meaning of 'branding' in your own words.

4. Explain why the writer has chosen to use the phrase 'Much more fizz!' to describe the rebranding of Brad's Drink as Pepsi-Cola.

5. What is the writer's attitude towards the person who thought of rebranding Royal Mail as 'Consignia'? Give evidence for your answer from the article.

6. The writer uses 'Hmm' to introduce information about the rebranding of Starbucks and Snickers. What does this mean and what does it tell us about the writer's attitude towards the rebranding of these companies?

7. Do you think the article is light-hearted or serious? Give evidence from the article in your answer.

8. How effective is the title 'Branding matters'? Give a reason for your answer.

9. How do you feel about branding, having read this article? Use evidence from the article in your answer.

Now assess your answers or assess your partner's answers. (The answers are on page 112. Don't look now!)

THINGS TO DO AND THINK ABOUT

Take some time to look back over this chapter. Remember that you were asked to assess your reading skills at the beginning of the chapter. What do you think about them now? Answer as honestly as you can.

Red means that you find the skill challenging (or are unsure what it means). Amber means that you need more practice in the skill. Green means that you are confident in the skill.

Reading skills	Red	Amber	Green
I can understand the ideas in the texts I read.			
I can analyse the texts I read.			
I can evaluate the texts I read.			

Make an 'action plan' to identify any aspect of reading you still want to work on:

Action	My plan
Area for improvement – for example, analysing	My area for improvement is …
Action – for example, revise, ask teacher for help, practise more …	I am going to …
Learning target – for example, to improve my analysing skills	This will improve …

KEY SKILL – LISTENING

LISTENING IN NATIONAL 4 ENGLISH

The focus in this chapter is on listening. Listening is one of the skills (or Outcomes) in the Analysis and Evaluation Unit. It is also one of the skills (or Outcomes) in the Literacy Unit. To achieve a pass in Listening (in English **and** Literacy) at National 4 level, you have to show you can listen to and understand spoken texts.

This chapter will help you to:

- understand what you listen to
- analyse what you listen to
- evaluate what you listen to.

LISTENING: WHAT SKILLS WILL I DEVELOP?

The Outcomes and Assessment Standards for listening in the Analysis and Evaluation Unit and in the Literacy Unit are shown side-by-side in the table below.

	Analysis and Evaluation Unit	Literacy Unit
Outcomes	2 Understand, analyse and evaluate straightforward spoken language by:	2 Listen to and understand straightforward spoken communication by:
Assessment Standards	2.1 Identifying the purpose and audience 2.2 Identifying the main idea and supporting details 2.3 Applying knowledge of language to explain meaning and effect	2.1 Selecting and using relevant information 2.2 Explaining aspects including audience and purpose 2.3 Commenting on effectiveness

LISTENING OUTCOMES AND ASSESSMENT STANDARDS EXPLAINED

So, to pass National 4 English, you need to show that you can:

UNDERSTAND SPOKEN TEXTS

To show that you understand spoken texts, you need to show that you know why the text has been created (**the purpose**) and who is likely to listen to it (**the audience**). You also need to show that you can find the **ideas** in a spoken text and explain **what** the text tells you.

In group discussion, you need to show that you understand the **purpose** of the discussion and that you respond appropriately and effectively to members of the group by using appropriate language.

ANALYSE SPOKEN TEXTS

Analysing a spoken text means commenting on the words, phrases, structures and ideas the speaker has used. You need to show that you understand **how** a text has been created. For example, you could be asked to explain why a speaker has chosen a particular word.

EVALUATE SPOKEN TEXTS

This means giving your opinion about **how well** a spoken text has been created. For example, you might be asked whether a speaker has presented a topic clearly, or whether the information is confusing. In group discussion, you could be asked to evaluate how well people contributed to the discussion.

LEARNING TOGETHER: Similarities And Differences

Turn to page 8 where the Outcomes and Assessment Standards for **reading** are explained. Can you spot similarities and differences between these and the Outcomes and Assessment Standards for **listening**? Take time to think, then write down the similarities and differences between the two. Now share these with your partner. What have you learned? Be prepared to share your ideas with the rest of the group/class.

 **ACTIVITY:** How Am I Doing?

Before you begin, think about how you rate your listening skills and fill in the grid below. Be honest! **Red** means that you find the skill challenging (or that you are unsure what it means). **Amber** means that you need more practice in the skill. **Green** means that you are confident in the skill.

ONLINE

Watch, and listen to, the film clip at www.bbc.co.uk/education/clips/z4jd7ty which is all about sound and hearing. It might give you some ideas to include in your listening diary.

Listening skills	Red	Amber	Green
I can understand a text I listen to.			
I can analyse a text I listen to.			
I can evaluate a text I listen to.			

BEING AWARE OF LISTENING

We listen every day to many different voices in many different contexts, including:

- teachers, parents and friends
- presenters and actors on TV
- radio and podcasts
- MP3 players
- online videos
- phone calls.

The list is endless!

 THINGS TO DO AND THINK ABOUT

Try a similar activity to the language diary mentioned in the introduction – but this time make it a listening diary. For a whole day, note down every spoken text you hear, starting from the moment you wake up. You will be surprised at the amount of language you come across and use every day. Look at these examples to help you get started.

Time	What I listened to
7.20	Mum calling me to get up
7.30	Watched and listened to breakfast TV
7.50	Listened to friend on phone
8.00	Listened to friend talking while walking to school
8.10…	

IMPROVING YOUR LISTENING

CONCENTRATION

One of the things we can all improve while we are listening is our concentration. Be honest – how many times have you been listening to a teacher and your mind has wandered off? Or how many times have you told a friend that you were listening to their every word but you were in fact only half-listening, or not really listening at all? Listening with full concentration to what is being said is called 'active listening'. There is more information about 'active listening' later in this chapter.

 **ACTIVITY**

Try listening with full concentration now. Turn off your phone, switch off your e-mail and focus. Ask your friend a question like 'What country would you most like to visit?' or 'Do you agree that we all need eight hours sleep a night?' Really concentrate on what he or she says. What did you learn?

LEARNING TOGETHER: Listening With Concentration

Work in a group of three. One is the **speaker**, one is the **listener** and one is the **observer**. The speaker chooses a topic, plans and prepares it and then talks about it for one minute without interruption. The listener listens silently to the speaker, but can use body language such as nodding or smiling. The listener should sit opposite the speaker. The observer watches the listener and the speaker.

After you have finished this activity, you should all think about and answer the questions below:

Speaker	Listener	Observer
How did it feel to be listened to for one minute?	How did it feel to listen for one minute without talking?	How well did the listener listen?
What did the listener do while listening that you liked?	What did you like about listening for one minute without talking?	What body language did the listener use?
What did the listener do while listening that you disliked?	What did you dislike about listening for one minute without talking?	What feedback would you give the speaker/listener?
What might you do differently next time?	What might you do differently next time?	What might you do differently next time?
Any other comments?	Any other comments?	Any other comments?

Now take turns so that everyone in the group of three has a chance to speak, listen and observe. Be prepared to share your experience with the rest of the group/class.

TYPES OF LISTENING

As you work through National 4 English, you will need to listen for information and to listen in group discussion. We'll have a look at each of these in more detail.

LISTENING FOR INFORMATION

This type of listening happens when you are listening to 'one voice' – for example, a teacher talking, a TV news report or an audio clip. When you are listening in school assembly, you are listening for information. For example, if your school assembly is a celebration of achievement, you might hear the name of a pupil who has taken part in a competition and some information about their achievements.

When you are developing your ability to listen for information, you need to respond in a way that shows you have understood this information. For example, you could listen to:

- a podcast and explain to a partner what you learned from the podcast
- a radio advertisement and suggest ways to improve the advertisement
- an online talk and create a mind map about the information in the talk
- another learner giving a presentation and summarise what they have said.

LISTENING IN GROUP DISCUSSION

This is a different type of 'listening for information'. When you listen in a discussion, you are hearing several people's views. So this type of listening means listening to more than one voice (and responding appropriately to what they say to show you have understood).

In any group discussion, you will:

- respond to show you understand others
- summarise what others say
- develop or build on what others say
- disagree (politely!) with what others say
- agree with what others say.

Doing any of these things shows that you understand what you are hearing in the discussion.

THINGS TO DO AND THINK ABOUT

Your listening skills will improve with practice. Try to listen carefully, rather than just having the radio or TV on in the background. Listen to a radio debate or watch and listen to TV or online discussions and interviews. Look out for opportunities to listen instead of reading – for example, you can listen to lots of short stories at the website http://www.thestoryplayer.com

There is a long list of texts on page 15 of this Study Guide. Look back at the list to remind yourself of the types of spoken texts you can listen to.

ONLINE

Check out the listening activity at http://www.learnenglishfeelgood.com/eslvideo/esl_movieclip6.html. This is a clip from the film *Moonrise Kingdom* with questions to answer. This is a straightforward introductory activity to listening for information. If you like the extract, you could watch the whole film.

ACTIVE LISTENING

Active listening means listening with full concentration. To listen actively, you need to prepare to listen, listen with full concentration, then check that you have understood what you have just listened to. Let's look at each of these steps in more detail:

PREPARE TO LISTEN

Think about what you are going to listen to. Before you listen, ask yourself the following questions:

- Are you physically prepared to listen?
- Are you able to see and hear clearly?
- Do you have pencil and paper ready to take notes?
- Who is the speaker?
- What do you know about the speaker?
- What is the topic?

- Work out your purpose for listening – what do you want to find out about the topic?
- What might the speaker say about the topic?
- What do you know already about this topic/title?
- What do you want to find out?

ACTIVITY: Fiction Or Non-Fiction?

When you are preparing to listen for information, you need to work out first whether it is a fiction or non-fiction text. Are you listening to a story, an extract from a play, a song or a factual text such as an online talk or radio programme?

Look at the listening examples below. Which are fiction and which are non-fiction?

- Song with the title *99 Red Balloons*.
- Sports commentator's comments about a football match.
- Horror film called *Power of the Dark*.
- Online talk with the title *Saving the Planet All By Myself*.
- Radio podcast about the best places to go mountain biking.
- TV advertisement for a new computer game.

Share your answers with your partner, then with the rest of your group/class.

LISTEN WITH FULL CONCENTRATION

Stay focused and listen actively to the text. Take notes or listen for specific ideas/ words/phrases and make sure that you can't be distracted.

During listening, think about the following questions:

- What are the main ideas about the topic?
- Are there any words/phrases/ideas that you don't understand?

When you are reading a text, you can highlight or underline words, phrases or ideas, but you obviously can't do this when you are listening. You therefore need to come up with a strategy to help you remember what is being said – for example, if you are listening to a recording, you can pause it or play parts of it again by rewinding. If you are listening 'live', you could note down words and phrases as you listen.

ONLINE

Listen to an online talk to practise active listening. Find a clip of your favourite sportsperson, actor or musician talking about their life. For example, Evelyn Glennie – a deaf Scottish musician – talks about how she hears music at http://www.bbc.co.uk/education/clips/zgqd7ty. Take regular pauses as you listen. At each pause, think about what has been said so far and think about what might be said next. At your next pause, check if your predictions were correct.

TASK 4

Now that you have observed the group discussion, complete the table below:

Name of group member _____	
Technique	**Example**
Repetition	
Intonation	
Emotive language	
Hyperbole	
Rule of three	
Alliteration	

Give the group member feedback by telling them:

- What you heard them say.
- What techniques they used.
- What they could do differently next time.

EVALUATING GROUP DISCUSSION

When you are asked to evaluate a group discussion, this means that you have to give your opinions about that discussion. You might be asked about:

- who contributed to the discussion
- the language and ideas in the discussion
- the main purpose of the discussion.

For example, you might be asked:

- Did the group agree or disagree and why?
- Was everyone involved equally?
- To what extent was the discussion clear?
- Did everyone contribute equally?
- Were key ideas missing from the discussion?

When you evaluate group discussion, you are judging how successful the group discussion was. As with

reading, you might be asked to comment on the purpose of the discussion – for example, is the purpose to:

- come to a decision?
- think about both sides of a topic or issue?
- produce or make something?
- share ideas?
- learn something?

So you could evaluate whether the group has achieved its purpose by asking the following questions.

Question	Yes	No	Comment
Did the group come to a decision?			
Did the group consider both sides of the argument equally?			
How well did the group work together to come to a decision?			
How well did the group share ideas? Did everyone make an equal contribution?			

LEARNING TOGETHER:
Evaluating Group Discussion

In your group, choose one of the following group discussion topics:

- Decide on a set of class rules.
- Should mobile phones be banned in school?
- Is a character from the class novel believable or not.
- Your choice of topic

Choose one group member to be an observer. Now take part in the discussion, while the observer watches and listens. After the group discussion, this person should evaluate the discussion using the table above. They can share this feedback with the group/class.

THINGS TO DO AND THINK ABOUT

Take some time to look back over this chapter. What do you think about your listening skills now? Answer as honestly as you can. Red means that you find the skill challenging (or are unsure what it means). Amber means that you need more practice in the skill. Green means that you are confident in the skill.

Listening for information

Listening skills	Red	Amber	Green
I can understand a text I listen to.			
I can analyse a text I listen to.			
I can evaluate a text I listen to.			

Listening in group discussion

Listening skills	Red	Amber	Green
I can understand what is said in a discussion.			
I can analyse contributions to a discussion.			
I can evaluate my role and others' roles in a discussion.			

Now make an 'action plan' to identify any aspect of listening you still want to work on. See the example plan on page 35.

KEY SKILL – WRITING

WRITING IN NATIONAL 4 ENGLISH

The focus in this chapter is on writing. Writing is one of the skills (or Outcomes) in the Creation and Production Unit. It is also one of the skills (or Outcomes) in the Literacy Unit. To achieve a pass in Writing (in English **and** Literacy) at National 4 level, you have to show that you can create texts in writing.

This chapter will help you to:

- choose ideas to include in your writing
- choose language for your writing
- organise your writing
- be technically accurate in your writing.

WRITING: WHAT SKILLS WILL I DEVELOP?

The Outcomes and Assessment Standards for writing in the Creation and Production Unit and in the Literacy Unit are shown side-by-side in the table below.

	Creation and Production Unit	**Literacy Unit**
Outcomes	1. Create and produce straightforward written texts by:	3. Write straightforward technically accurate texts by:
Assessment Standards	1.1 Selecting ideas and content, using a format and structure appropriate to purpose and audience 1.2 Applying knowledge of language in terms of language choice and technical accuracy 1.3 Communicating meaning at first reading	3.1 Selecting and using appropriate language 3.2 Organising writing appropriately 3.3 Using appropriate spelling, punctuation and grammar

WRITING OUTCOMES AND ASSESSMENT STANDARDS EXPLAINED

So, to pass National 4 English, you need to show that you can do the following:

CHOOSE APPROPRIATE IDEAS

This means that your ideas have to 'suit' the text you are writing. For example, if you are writing about a personal experience, your ideas will be about what you did and how this made you feel. If you are writing an application letter for a Saturday job, you will write about your experience and skills.

CHOOSE WORDS AND PHRASES THAT ARE APPROPRIATE FOR THE PIECE OF WRITING

For example, if your Headteacher wrote a glowing letter describing your amazing achievements, they would use the word 'child' not 'kid' and 'excellent' but definitely not 'awesome'!

ORGANISE YOUR WRITING

To make your writing clear and easy to follow, you need to organise it. That means deciding on a structure and well-ordered paragraphs. (The structure will obviously depend on what type of text you are writing.)

COMMUNICATE MEANING AT FIRST READING

Your writing has to make sense when someone else reads it. If you write accurately with all the correct punctuation, spelling and expression this will make it much easier for your reader to follow what you are writing.

HOW MUCH DO I HAVE TO WRITE?

Different texts have different lengths. The important thing to remember is that the length should suit the audience you are writing for. For example, if you are writing a story for young children, your text will be shorter than if you are writing a novel for teenagers.

However, when your writing is being assessed for the National 4 English Literacy Unit, you need to write more than 300 words – so it is a good idea to get used to what more than 300 words looks like and how long this takes you to write.

 **ACTIVITY:** How Am I Doing?

Before you begin, think about how you rate your writing skills and fill in the grid below. Be honest! **Red** means that you find the skill challenging (or are unsure what it means). **Amber** means that you need more practice in the skill. **Green** means you are confident in this skill.

Writing skills	Red	Amber	Green
I can use appropriate ideas in my writing.			
I can use appropriate language in my writing.			
I can use appropriate structures for my writing.			
I write clearly so that someone else can understand my writing.			

GETTING STARTED

Many learners find it difficult to get started when writing. A blank page can be quite scary or quite exciting ... How do **you** feel when you have a blank page in front of you?

Here are some tips to help you to get started:

- Get into the habit of writing every day – even if it's just for a few minutes. A short entry in a diary is a good idea.
- Carry a notebook with you and write down your ideas. You could write what you see, something you have to remember to buy, something you hear... anything. Again, the idea is to get you used to writing.
- Work out the time of day when you find writing easiest. Sometimes writing is easier later on in the day but some writers start very early. Try writing at different times of day and see which you prefer.
- When you are writing for yourself, don't worry about spelling or punctuation. If you are keeping a diary, it only has to make sense to you – it doesn't matter about anyone else!
- When you have written something, leave it for a while. The important thing is to get an idea down on paper – then you can work on improving it later.

 **DON'T FORGET**

Enjoy yourself! Write a silly poem or make up a rap. Have fun with your writing.

 THINGS TO DO AND THINK ABOUT

Check out the website www.bigthink.com. Enter 'Getting started with writing' into the website search box. There are lots of clips of famous writers (such as Stephen Fry) talking about how they get started with writing.

THE STAGES OF WRITING

Very few people write a perfect piece at the first attempt. Most writers work through the stages below:

1. planning 2. drafting 3. revising 4. feedback 5. publishing

You might have to go back and do the 'revising/feedback' stages a few times before you are happy with your writing.

Let's look at these stages in more detail:

STAGE 1: PLANNING

You can write a shopping list or a quick e-mail or text without planning it. But if you are writing a longer text – for example, a report, a letter or an essay – **planning** will always improve your final writing.

You can plan in a number of ways. You could draw a mind map, make some notes, jot down a rough paragraph plan or talk through your ideas with someone else. If you do this, you'll have fewer changes to make when you actually start writing.

DON'T FORGET

Planning includes thinking about your ideas and how you are going to organise them. Many famous writers plan 'in their heads' in this way – as well as writing notes or creating mind maps. The key thing is to think before your write!

STAGE 2: DRAFTING

When you are **drafting**, you are simply writing down your ideas in the form of words, phrases and sentences as they come to you. Later, you can choose the perfect word to describe something or the best position for a particular word.

⚙ **ACTIVITY:** Quick Write

Time yourself for this activity. Give yourself one minute to write about any topic. (You can think about and plan your ideas before you write.)

You can choose from the topics below or choose one of your own. No need to correct any mistakes … just write whatever comes into your head!

- A bouquet of flowers
- My proudest moment
- A summer holiday
- A sports car
- My hero/heroine
- Keeping fit and healthy

JUST A WEE NOTE

John Steinbeck, the famous American writer who wrote *Of Mice and Men* (see page 32) said 'Write as freely and rapidly as possible and throw the whole thing on paper. Never correct or rewrite until the whole thing is down.' Good advice!

JUST A WEE NOTE

If you keep all your 'quick writes' and rough ideas in a notebook, you can look back at them. You never know when one of your 'quick writes' could become a longer piece of writing – perhaps the beginning of a story or an idea for a blog!

STAGE 3: REVISING

Revising your writing means doing two things: **proofreading** and **redrafting**. What's the difference?

REVISING – PROOFREADING

This means making changes to your punctuation, spelling and grammar. This is sometimes called checking for 'technical accuracy'. The Outcome for writing in the Literacy Unit – 'Write straightforward technically accurate texts' – means that your writing has to have correct spelling, punctuation and grammar. So it is important to check that your writing makes sense.

DON'T FORGET

The text that you write for the Literacy Unit is likely to be a non-fiction text, such as a report. It has to be more than 300 words long – so remember to check the word length as well as proofreading and redrafting it.

Ask yourself these five questions when you are proofreading your writing (or looking at your partner's writing):

Proofreading questions	Yes/No	Comment
Do my sentences make sense?		
Have I checked my spelling?		
Have I checked my punctuation?		
Have I checked my grammar?		
Have I missed out anything?		
Is the writing an appropriate length?		

REVISING – REDRAFTING

This means re-reading the text and changing words and phrases to improve your writing. You might want to change whole sentences and/or paragraphs, or change the order or organisation of your writing.

Ask yourself these ten questions when you are redrafting your writing (or looking at your partner's writing):

Redrafting questions	Yes/No	Comment
Have I done what I was asked?		
Does my writing make sense?		
Is my purpose clear?		
Is there anything I could add or take out?		
Have I organised my writing clearly?		
Is my introduction clear?		
Is my conclusion clear?		
Are the paragraphs linked/do the paragraphs 'flow'?		
Is my writing interesting? (What would make it better?)		
Could I improve any words or phrases?		

STAGE 4: FEEDBACK

Look at the comments below. Which of these areas do you need to work on? What kinds of comments has the teacher or your partner made about your writing?

Feedback/comment from your readers	Advice
You could make your writing more interesting. Your sentences are very short! Try to link sentences together. Your writing isn't exciting.	Don't worry! Read the 'Spice up your writing' section on page 54
Your story is muddled. Where are your paragraphs? I'm confused! Your writing doesn't make sense.	Read the 'Express yourself clearly' section on page 54
Write in sentences! Make sure you use capital letters and full stops. Check over your punctuation. You have spelled some words wrongly.	Read the 'Write it right' section on page 54

Feedback On Your Writing

First think of something to write, then write it. It could be one of the 'quick writes' above, something you have written for another subject, a letter or any other text.

Now work with your partner. Ask them to read what you have written. Have a look at the questions above and tell your partner one aspect of your writing that you want them to focus on. For example, you might want feedback on whether you have organised your writing clearly and, if not, how you could improve this. Or you could ask your partner to give you feedback on your punctuation.

Your partner will then do the same for you.

Be prepared to share your ideas with the rest of the group/class.

STAGE 5: PUBLISHING

Publishing your writing can mean creating a final version, showing your writing to others or displaying your writing (perhaps in a school newspaper, in a classroom display or online). It can also mean printing and selling your book to the general public!

You could:

- mount your writing on backing paper
- illustrate your writing with pictures and/or diagrams
- create a 'book' with a front and back cover
- create a title page with the title, your name and the date
- type up your writing or write it out neatly

 ONLINE

There are a lot of good online word games you can play to improve your word power. Try challenging a friend to a game of *Words with Friends* or *Lexulous* or *Words by Post*. Enter these titles into any search engine.

 DON'T FORGET

A word of warning – many learners draft, redraft and redraft endlessly! Why not write a rough draft, get some feedback on it and redraft once? This can be more effective than endless redrafting.

 THINGS TO DO AND THINK ABOUT

Why not create a flow diagram or mind map which shows the five stages of writing (look at page 52!) – you could display these in your classroom.

IMPROVING YOUR WRITING

SPICE UP YOUR WRITING

- **Add in words** – at the beginning, in the middle or at the end.
- **Improve words** – replace a single word with a better word.
- **Play with words** – use techniques like similes, metaphors and alliteration.

Have a go at improving the boring sentence 'I ran to school' by using one of the ideas above. Here's one example of each technique to get you started:

- Add in words: *At around 8 am, I ran quickly to school, my shirt flapping and papers flying out of my schoolbag.*
- Improve words: *I dashed to school*
- Play with words: *I ran rapidly to school*

EXPRESS AND ORGANISE YOUR IDEAS CLEARLY

Express and organise your ideas clearly by using **linking words and phrases** and **paragraphs**.

LINKING WORDS AND PHRASES

Use linking words and phrases to make your ideas clear and to help your sentences to flow:

but	only	although	if	however	as well as	while
since	finally	in fact	so	so that	because	

PARAGRAPHS

A paragraph is a group of sentences about one main idea or topic.

A paragraph:

- usually has around five or six sentences
- usually has a topic sentence (a main sentence somewhere in the paragraph that states the main idea)
- usually has a conclusion that finishes off the paragraph and/or links to the next paragraph.

Remember to start a new paragraph when you want to:

- begin a new idea or make a new point
- change the setting in fiction writing – for example, move from beach to town
- end your introduction or start a conclusion.

WRITE IT RIGHT

Look at the table on the next page and make sure that you understand each of these punctuation marks and why/when they are used.

ONLINE

Watch the video at http://www.engvid.com/how-to-increase-your-vocabulary This is a video for non-native speakers of English, but it has some great advice about increasing your vocabulary (and some advice about grammar too).

ONLINE

Try out any of the activities at www.bbc.co.uk/bitesize/ks3/english/reading/sentences/revision/1/ to help you with writing sentences.

ONLINE

There is lots of information about paragraphs at www.time4writing.com/writing-resources/paragraph-writing-secrets/

JUST A WEE NOTE

Did you know there is an International Apostrophe Day? Find out about it by doing some online research – and why the apostrophe is an important punctuation mark!

Punctuation mark	Looks like...	Mainly used	Example
Apostrophe	'	-To show that something belongs to something or someone -To show a missing letter	The boy's shoes I can't come to the meeting after school.
Colon	:	-To elaborate on an idea – one way to do this is to introduce a list -Before a quotation	Remember to pack: shorts, socks, a hat, gloves and a first aid kit. J K Rowling wrote: 'Harry Potter was a highly unusual boy in many ways.'
Comma	,	-In lists -To separate clauses -In direct speech	Please bring tea, coffee, milk and juice. The cat, tired and wet, sat in front of the fire. 'I saw him earlier,' she said.
Exclamation mark	!	-At the end of a sentence to show an exclamation -At the end of a sentence to show something is said loudly	'Well done!' 'Come inside right now!' shouted his mother.
Full stop	.	-Marks the end of a sentence -Shows that a word has been abbreviated (shortened)	Dolphins are very intelligent animals. Prof. (Professor)
Inverted commas (or speech marks)	' or "	-To show direct speech -To show a quotation	"Why did you do that?" he asked. The Queen said she was 'absolutely delighted'. The poem is called 'A Leaf Lay Dying'.
Question mark	?	-At the end of a sentence to show a question	Why am I always late? How do I open this?
semi-colon	;	-To show a break which is stronger than a comma	I wanted to tell him what I thought; I marched up to his door.
Dash	–	-To show a break	I was going to buy the shoes – and then I changed my mind!
Brackets	( )	-Around extra information or explanation	Greig ran towards the football pitch as usual

ONLINE

There is a fun video at www.bbc.co.uk/education/clips/zth4d2p about how punctuation helps to make meaning clear.

CHECK YOUR SPELLING

Are you confused by 'there, their and they're'? Can you spell 'necessary'? Do you know the difference between 'affect' and 'effect'?

When you come across a new word **always** use the LOOK – COVER – WRITE – CHECK method.

- LOOK at the new word for as long as you need.
- COVER the word and close your eyes.
- Now open your eyes and WRITE the word down without looking back at it.
- CHECK to see if you're right.

Remember rules for tricky spellings. For example, there is **a rat** in sep**arat**e!

THINGS TO DO AND THINK ABOUT

Everyone writes a text, for example, a web page entry. The class then divides into three groups:

Group 1 – gives feedback on the words/language you have used.
Group 2 – gives feedback on the organisation/structure you have used.
Group 3 – gives feedback on the spelling and punctuation you have used.

DON'T FORGET

Even if you use a spellchecker, you still need to know which word is the appropriate one from the options you are given.

ONLINE

The webpage at http://www.bbc.co.uk/bitesize/standard/english/writing/general_advice/revision/3/ has advice about paragraphs, punctuation and some helpful spelling videos.

ONLINE

Make a word search with words you find difficult to spell. You can create your own wordsearch at http://puzzlemaker.discoveryeducation.com/WordSearchSetupForm.asp

CREATING TEXTS 1

FOUR MOST COMMON TYPES OF WRITING

This chapter gives advice about the four most common types of writing:

- creative
- personal
- factual
- persuasive

There is advice to help you get started on each type of writing. You will also learn about what ideas to include, what language to use and how to structure each type of writing. We'll start with creative writing.

WHAT IS CREATIVE WRITING?

Creative writing:

- is made up (although it can be based on things that have happened or that are true)
- includes description
- uses creative language.

The main purposes of creative writing are to:

- explore ideas, feelings and emotions (for example, through characters)
- entertain the reader.

⚙ ACTIVITY

In this section, you are going to work on writing a story. Creative writing includes poetry and plays too, so once you have written your story, try writing a poem or a play using the same theme.

THE RECIPE FOR A SUCCESSFUL STORY

Think of a story as a recipe. The ingredients for your story are:

- characters
- setting
- plot
- theme
- language

If you want your story to turn out successfully, you need to use all the ingredients in the recipe. Think about it. A story isn't a story without characters. If a story has no plot, nothing will happen.

We'll look at each of these five 'ingredients' in detail over the next few pages.

CHARACTERS

Stories usually have only one or two main characters. In *The Fault in our Stars* by John Green, the two main characters fall in love, while in *The Curious Incident of the Dog in the Night-time* by Mark Haddon, there is one main character who tells the story. You can include other characters, of course, but choose one or two characters to focus on.

You can develop a character by thinking about their:

Name		**Ebenezer Scrooge** Charles Dickens used some great names for his characters – for example, Bumble, Scrooge, Oliver Twist. Try to think of names that 'fit' your characters.
Appearance		What does your character look like and sound like? How are they dressed?
Personality		What type of person is your character? Kind, sarcastic, a bully, caring, wise, lively?
Background		Where was your character born? What is your character's family like?
Relationships		Who are the character's family and friends? How well does your character get along with others?
Actions		What will the character say and do in your story? Will they make mistakes, interact with others, make decisions?

⚙ ACTIVITY: Talking About A Character

Have you seen any of the *Toy Story* films? There are three main characters: Woody, Jessie and Buzz Lightyear. Choose your favourite character. Share with a partner what you know about the character you have chosen. (If you haven't seen *Toy Story*, you can choose another film and follow the same process.)

Use the headings in the table above to help you – for example:

- What does Jessie look like?
- How does she act?
- Who does she relate to?
- What does she say and do in the film?

DON'T FORGET

In a way, all writing is creative because you create the text in your head and then write it down. In this Study Guide, we will use the term 'creative writing' to mean fiction writing.

SETTING

Setting means where and when a story is set. Your story could be set in New York in the 1920s, in Glasgow during World War Two or in Plockton right now! Decide on your setting before you start writing. Your story can have more than one setting. You could start off the story in Irvine in the future but include a 'flashback' to another time and place. Your story could be about a journey starting in St Andrews and ending in Dundee.

 **ACTIVITY:** Match The Title To The Genre

Your setting will be closely linked to the **genre** of your story. For example, you might choose the setting of a haunted castle for a horror story. When you go into your school or local library, you will see many different genres. In fact, books are often arranged according to genre.

Look at the Fiction Section bookshelf below. The titles and genres are all mixed up. Draw a bookshelf, but this time put the correct genre names above the correct titles.

FICTION SECTION

Romance

Science fiction & fantasy

Horror

Historical fiction

Detective & crime

 **ACTIVITY:** Get To Know The Features Of A Genre

If you want to write a specific genre of story, try reading some examples. That way, you will get to know the features of the genre. For example, in a 'western' there are usually cowboys and Native Americans, horses, fights and shoot-outs! What are the features of a romance or a detective/crime novel?

PLOT

Always think about what will happen in your story before you start writing. Your story should have a shape. The shape of a story is usually an arc.

Start your story with a 'conflict' such as a meeting, an argument, a relationship or a mystery. Then develop this idea and build up the tension to the climax – the most important, exciting or shocking part of your story. You then explain anything the reader doesn't know towards the end of the story and finish it off.

EXAMPLE

Hansel and Gretel

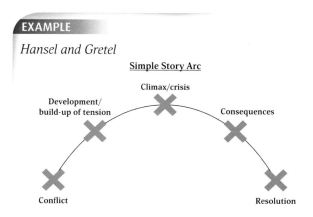

Simple Story Arc

Conflict – Hansel and Gretel leave home to look for food.

Development/build-up of tension – they arrive at a gingerbread house. An old woman takes them prisoner.

Climax/crisis – the children push the old woman into the oven.

Consequences – the children escape.

Resolution – the children return home and live happily ever after.

 ONLINE

Try out the title generator at http://novelistvmd.awardspace.com which generates random titles for romance and western novels!

 LEARNING TOGETHER: Story Arc

With your partner, choose a fairy tale such as *Cinderella* or *Little Red Riding Hood*. Think on your own first about the shape of the fairy tale. Then discuss the shape with your partner and create a story arc for it, writing beside the arc what happens at each point in the fairy tale. Be prepared to share your ideas with the rest of your group/class.

 THINGS TO DO AND THINK ABOUT

Do some research into a setting you are thinking about using for a story. For example, if you want to set your story in a funfair, then read about funfairs and, if possible, visit one so that you can include some realistic details in your story. Likewise, you could research the 'roaring twenties' or the 'swinging sixties' so you can include details to make your story more realistic.

CREATING TEXTS 2

THE RECIPE FOR A SUCCESSFUL SHORT STORY (CONTD.)

Now we're going to look at the final two ingredients – theme and language.

THEME

The theme of a story (or poem or play) is the 'big idea' that it's trying to put across. This is sometimes called the 'moral' or 'message' of the story. To work out the theme, ask yourself the question 'What is this text telling me about?' For example, the theme might be:

- money can't buy happiness
- being an outsider
- don't judge people on appearances
- power
- we should take care of our environment
- the importance of family.

 ACTIVITY

Look at the list of novel titles and blurbs below. (The 'blurb' is the description of a novel, usually on the back cover.) What do you think the theme of each novel might be? Choose **one** from the two suggestions given ... and be prepared to give reasons why you think this might be the theme.

One Day in Paradise

Title	Blurb	Theme?
One Day in Paradise	Sam and Erin were looking forward to their dream holiday. But something goes badly wrong before it starts ...	Coping with challenges OR Love
Billy's Battle	When a motorway is planned which will run right through the family's farmland, Billy makes a life-changing decision ...	The environment OR Conflict
Aldura, land of war	In the land of Aldura, who will inherit the throne from King Malvon when he dies? And who will decide?	Family OR Hate

LANGUAGE

Language is the final ingredient in a successful story. It's so important that we're going to cover it in detail over the next few pages.

The secret of a great story is to use great words and phrases. And if you use techniques to make these words and phrases even more interesting, then you'll be well on the way to a really great story that people will want to read.

 ACTIVITY: Building Up Your Vocabulary

One of the easiest ways to improve your writing is to use better words and phrases. Use a thesaurus to help you do this. There will be one in your library, or you can access one online. For example, if you look up 'rain' in a thesaurus (for example: http://thesaurus.com) you will find:

drizzle   flood   monsoon   storm   shower   torrent

Look up the following words in a thesaurus. Can you find five words as alternatives for each of these words?

went   love   many   nice   said

ACTIVITY: Reading A Short Story Extract

TASK 1

Read the extract on the next page about Dana and her friend, Caitlin, who run a restaurant. Dana has fallen down the stairs and is in hospital.

 DON'T FORGET

Writers don't usually tell you what the theme of a story is. You have to work this out from what the characters do and say and what happens to them.

 ONLINE

You can type your writing into www.writewords.org.uk/word_count.asp The counter will tell you how many times you have used a word. If you have repeated a word over and over again, perhaps you could improve your writing by finding alternative words?

Dana was dreaming. She was back in the yard behind the cycle shop; she felt the rain pattering on her face and the hardness of the cobbles against her back. She was colder, colder than she had ever been; in fact, so cold that numbness was creeping up her body. When the numbness reaches my heart I'll be dead and I don't want to die, she found herself thinking. They'll be so distressed if I die and I'll be no use to anyone. How will poor Caitlin manage with the restaurant still not finished? I simply must move, try to sit up, call for help! She turned her head a little and a sharp pain stabbed from the back of her neck to the top of her head, making her wince and long to cry out, but when she opened her mouth no sound emerged and rain fell in. She moved her head again, more cautiously this time, and the pain arrowed through her, from her neck to the back of her eyes, and did not stop for some seconds after she had frozen into immobility once more.

Later, she could not tell how much, she opened her eyes, but saw only the grey sky above and the steadily falling rain. Then there was darkness, and a voice she did not know saying words she could not recognise; they might have been in a foreign language for all she could tell.

Later still, she woke again to a rocking motion, and to hear another unknown voice saying something about concussion. She tried to open her eyes, to speak, but her lids seemed glued shut and her mouth would not obey her command to open. Terror seized her. Where was she? *Who* was she?

(Extract from *The Runaway* by Katie Flynn, Arrow books)

TASK 1

This extract comes from *The Runaway* by Katie Flynn. Pair and share with a partner – discuss **either** what you think will happen in the novel based on what happens in this extract **or** think of an alternative title for the novel based on what happens in this extract.

THINGS TO DO AND THINK ABOUT

When you are writing a description about something, imagine that you are taking a photograph of what you see. Imagine that you 'zoom in' on one person, one place or one object. Use detailed language to describe everything you can see in the 'zoom'.

TASK 2

There is some great description in this extract which helps you to picture what is happening to Dana. For example, 'She tried to open her eyes, to speak, but her lids seemed glued shut and her mouth would not obey her command to open'. With your partner, identify another two descriptions in this extract which help you to picture clearly what is happening to her.

TASK 3

Your next task is to try to come up with some great descriptions of your own. With your partner, choose a photograph or a picture of a famous painting.

'Zoom in' on one person, place or object in the photograph and write a detailed description of it. Describe this part of the photograph to your partner in as much detail as you can.

Your partner will then 'zoom in' on another person, place or object in the photograph, write a detailed description of it and describe it to you in as much detail as they can.

Be prepared to share your writing with the rest of your group/class.

CREATING TEXTS 3

Let's look more closely at some of the techniques Katie Flynn has used to give her writing 'sparkle'.

USING REPETITION

Instead of writing 'Dana was cold', she writes 'She was colder, colder than she had ever been; in fact, so cold that numbness was creeping up her body'. Notice how she uses 'colder' and 'cold' three times in one sentence to emphasise how cold Dana is.

USING THE FIVE SENSES

Look at the table below. It shows how you can use the five senses in your writing to make it 'sparkle'.

Sense	Ask yourself ...	Examples
Touch	What is the character touching or what can the character feel? What does it feel like? What texture is it?	rough smooth spiky dry slippery fuzzy icy rocky feathery
Taste	What can a character taste? Does it taste pleasant or unpleasant?	sour sweet bitter salty minty bland
Hearing	What can the character hear? What sounds or noises are there?	shrill faint soft high-pitched squeaking hissing
Sight	What can a character see? What type of landscape/interior is it?	dull elegant beautiful sparkling dirty bright clear colourful wooden
Smell	What can a character smell? Is it pleasant or unpleasant?	rotten earthy flowery mouldy stale fragrant burnt

LEARNING TOGETHER:
The Five Senses

TASK 1

In the extract from *The Runaway*, the writer uses three of these five senses: touch, hearing and sight. Read the extract over again. Can you find examples of each of the five senses? One example has been done for you. Give as many examples as you can for each sense. Quote the words the writer uses. Discuss these with your partner.

What does Dana **touch**?	She feels/touches ...
What does Dana **hear**?	She hears ...
What does Dana **see**?	She sees 'the grey sky above'.

Share your examples with the rest of the group.

TASK 2

Now, with your partner, think of how the writer could have added the other two senses – taste and smell.

- What might Dana taste? For example, rain fell into her mouth – what do you think the rain might taste like? Work with your partner to write a sentence to add to the extract using taste.
- What might Dana smell? For example, she was in the yard behind the bicycle shop in her dream – what do you think she might smell? Work with your partner to write a sentence to add to the extract using smell.

DON'T FORGET

You don't have to use all five senses in your writing. Choose the ones that 'fit' your story best. For example, you could describe what a character or object looks like **or** you could describe the sounds a character can hear.

TASK 3

Close your eyes. Imagine walking along a beach in summer:

What can you **see**?	Are there people there? What are they doing? What are they wearing? Where are they? What colours are there? What do the shapes look like?
What can you **hear**?	What sounds are there? The sounds of water? Shouting? The wind? Music? What are the sounds like?
What can you **touch**?	What can you feel under your feet? On your skin? What do the sand and waves feel like?
What can you **taste**?	What is there to eat? Can you taste salt? Or something else?
What can you **smell**?	What can you smell? Salt water? Coconut? Is it pleasant or unpleasant? What are the smells like?

Now open your eyes. Write down, in as much detail as you can, everything about this scene from the images you created in your mind.

TASK 4

Use your five senses to write a description of one of the below:

- a crowd at a sporting event – for example, a football match
- a fireworks display
- a school playground in winter
- your pet
- a photograph or a picture of a scene of your own choice

(Remember to 'zoom in' on the scene so you can describe it in detail.)

USING IMAGERY

Imagery is when you create pictures or images in your reader's mind with your words. Similes and metaphors are examples of imagery.

A metaphor compares something with something else that is usually very different. For example, 'That boy is a monkey!' compares the boy's physical actions and behaviour to those of a monkey – can you picture in your mind the boy leaping about and misbehaving just like a cheeky monkey?

A simile compares something with something else using 'like' or 'as'. For example, Lennie, a character in *Of Mice and Men*, is described as '... snorting into the water like a horse'. Can you picture in your mind the image of Lennie slurping up the water like a big, thirsty horse?

THINGS TO DO AND THINK ABOUT

Look at the video at https://www.youtube.com/watch?v=KfeqRTMBm5A called *Similes from songs and movies*. You can listen here to lots of examples of similes – from Duran Duran to Beyonce!

CREATING TEXTS 4

USING ONOMATOPOEIA

Onomatopoeia is a technique where a writer uses a word that describes the sound it makes – for example, 'bacon sizzled in the frying pan'. There are many examples of onomatopoeia such as *smack*, *thud*, *thump*, *bang*, *crash*, *buzz* and *hiss*.

We are going to look at examples of onomatopoeia and imagery in *A Case of Murder* by Vernon Scannell. In this poem, a nine-year-old boy is at home alone, and is so frightened of his cat that he kills it and then hides it. First, read the poem.

 LEARNING TOGETHER:
Onomatopoeia And Imagery

TASK 1

There are lots of examples of onomatopoeia in the poem – 'purr' is one. Can you find **five** other examples? Read the poem over again, and when you have found five examples, work with your partner and compare your answers. Did you find the same five examples? Agree on which example you like best and why. Be prepared to share your ideas with the rest of the group/class.

TASK 2

The table below gives you some examples of similes and metaphors from the poem.

Type of image	Example	Comment
Simile	round eyes mad as gold plump as a cushion quick as a sudden crack in glass cracked like a nut	The cat is plump – perhaps lazy. Well-padded, fat – well-fed, smug? Cushion shape – round, filled out.
Metaphor	A buzzing machine of soft black stuff the wound of fear gaped wide and raw hot blood in a muff He dared not touch the thing with his hands	Muff is fur hand warmer, comforting –horrible image of hot blood instead of hands. As if the animal is a thing without feelings.

Choose **one** simile and **one** metaphor. Can you explain what you think they mean? Make some notes on each image. Two have been done for you as examples. Be prepared to share your ideas with the group/class.

A Case of Murder

They should not have left him there alone,
Alone that is except for the cat.
He was only nine, not old enough
To be left alone in a basement flat,
Alone, that is, except for the cat.
A dog would have been a different thing,
A big gruff dog with slashing jaws,
But a cat with round eyes mad as gold,
Plump as a cushion with tucked-in paws---
Better have left him with a fair-sized rat!
But what they did was leave him with a cat.
He hated that cat; he watched it sit,
A buzzing machine of soft black stuff,
He sat and watched and he hated it,
Snug in its fur, hot blood in a muff,
And its mad gold stare and the way it sat
Crooning dark warmth: he loathed all that.
So he took Daddy's stick and he hit the cat.
Then quick as a sudden crack in glass
It hissed, black flash, to a hiding place
In the dust and dark beneath the couch,
And he followed the grin on his new-made face,
A wide-eyed, frightened snarl of a grin,
And he took the stick and he thrust it in,
Hard and quick in the furry dark.
The black fur squealed and he felt his skin
Prickle with sparks of dry delight.
Then the cat again came into sight,
Shot for the door that wasn't quite
But the boy, quick too, slammed fast the door:
The cat, half-through, was cracked like a nut
And the soft black thud was dumped on the floor.
Then the boy was suddenly terrified
And he bit his knuckles and cried and cried;
But he had to do something with the dead thing there.
His eyes squeezed beads of salty prayer
But the wound of fear gaped wide and raw;
He dared not touch the thing with his hands
So he fetched a spade and shovelled it
And dumped the load of heavy fur
In the spidery cupboard under the stair
Where it's been for years, and though it died
It's grown in that cupboard and its hot low **purr**
Grows slowly louder year by year:
There'll not be a corner for the boy to hide
When the cupboard swells and all sides split
   And the huge black cat pads out of it.

LEARNING TOGETHER: Time To Create A Text!

The next activity will bring together everything you have learned about the ingredients of a successful story.

With your partner, look at the suggestions below and choose one (or more) **characters**, a **setting** (place), a **setting** (time), a **plot**, a **theme** and an **opening**. There is an extra column for you to add your own ideas if you want.

Character	Mother, aged 45	Girl, aged 17	Young child, aged 6	Boy, aged 15	Grandfather, aged 78	Twins, aged 14	
Setting – place	Ruined castle	Housing estate	Outer space	City centre	Deserted village	Camp-site	
Setting – time	The present day	Last year	The future	Victorian times	World war two	The Stone Age	
Plot	An argument leads to a fight …	A stranger arrives with good news …	A valuable painting is stolen …	A storm destroys a community …	A day out ends in disaster…	A family member leaves home…	
Theme	Lost love	Good versus bad	Growing up	Power	Loneliness	Friendship	
Opening	"I was completely terrified …"	"'No-one tells me what to do!'…"	"He/she stepped quietly through the doorway…"	"Pale and shaking, he/she looked up to see …"	"The grass was still wet when I …"	"'I can't believe it …'"	

Add the ideas you have chosen together to create a story. For example, you could start your story with:

'I can't believe it!' shouted my mum. 'There's a reporter and a TV crew outside because we've won the lottery!'

Why not go further and create your own digital story using still photographs, moving images, words and sounds. There's a great example of a digital story – *Inanimate Alice* – at www.inanimatealice.com/

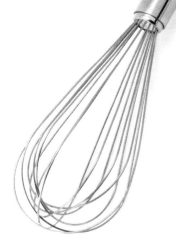

JUST A WEE NOTE

mother, aged 45
girl, aged 17
housing estate
the present day
a stranger arrives with good
news …
growing up
'I can't believe it …'

 THINGS TO DO AND THINK ABOUT

When you have finished this activity (or any other activity in National 4 English, ask yourself the following:

- **WWW** – What went well? (Give one success.)
- **EBI** – Even better if... (Give one way you could improve your writing next time.)

You can either assess yourself this way or read someone else's writing and give them at least one WWW and one EBI.

PERSONAL WRITING 1

WHAT IS PERSONAL WRITING?

Personal writing:

- is about your experience
- includes descriptions of your experiences
- includes your feelings/emotions about the experiences
- includes your reflections now about the experiences.

The main purposes of personal writing are to:

- explain something that happened
- reflect on the experience
- entertain the reader.

Although creative writing usually refers to stories, poems and plays, don't forget that personal writing is also creative. This is because you will use language creatively in your personal writing to describe and reflect. Read on to find out how!

HOW TO BEGIN

Beginning a piece of personal writing is often the most difficult part. The following activity will help you get started.

LEARNING TOGETHER: Writing About Memories

You are going to write about your memories of childhood and growing up. You could choose to write about one specific event – for example, taking part in a dance show when you were five or playing your first football game at seven. Or you could write about several things that happened to you at a certain age – for example, you might have started primary school, moved house **and** broken your arm when you were five!

TASK 2

Now choose a memory to share with your partner – for example, your first day at primary school. Describe this memory to them. Try to include details about what you saw, tasted, heard, smelt and touched. Be prepared to share your ideas with the rest of the group/class.

DON'T FORGET

Remember the three top tips for personal writing:
-write about how you felt
-describe what happened
-reflect on your experience.

THINGS TO DO AND THINK ABOUT

When you have completed your personal writing, share it with a partner. When you have read your partner's work, give them a feedback sandwich! It works like this:

Slice of bread - Make a positive comment on the writing.

Sandwich filling - Suggest one thing which could be improved (and an explanation of **how** to improve it).

Slice of bread - Make a positive comment on the writing.

FACTUAL WRITING

WHAT IS FACTUAL WRITING?

Factual writing:

- includes facts, information and statistics
- uses clear straightforward language
- includes technical words.

The main purposes of factual writing are to:

- give information
- describe something
- explain something – for example, how to make or do something.

Some examples of factual writing are:

- recipes
- letters
- leaflets
- instructions
- reports
- textbooks
- newspaper and magazine articles.

We are going to look in more detail at factual writing in leaflets. These:

- are usually divided into sections or paragraphs
- are written in straightforward, factual style
- often contain headlines and sub-headings
- often contain pictures and graphics.

Here's an example of a one-page leaflet:

ONLINE →

Check out http://www. bbc.co.uk/schools/ gcsebitesize/english/writing/ writingtoinformrev2.shtml which explains the differences between describing, informing and explaining.

EXAMPLE

This leaflet contains:

- numbered points
- bold type
- a heading
- an illustration
- information
- a clear purpose – to make motorists aware of cyclists.

LEARNING TOGETHER:
Evaluate The Leaflet

How could this leaflet be improved? Would more illustrations or a photograph improve it? What information would you add or leave out? Would you use a different layout or heading?

Imagine you have been asked to write a second page for this leaflet. Think about what would you include and why. Share your ideas with your partner. Working with your partner, now create this second page. This is an opportunity to make all the improvements you have suggested! Be prepared to share your ideas with the rest of the group/class.

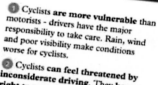

WHAT CYCLISTS WOULD LIKE MOTORISTS TO KNOW

1 Cyclists **are more vulnerable** than motorists - drivers have the major responsibility to take care. Rain, wind and poor visibility make conditions worse for cyclists.

2 Cyclists **can feel threatened by inconsiderate driving**. They **have a right to space** on the road and need <u>extra</u> room at junctions and roundabouts where cars change speed, position and direction.

3 Cyclists **ride away from the kerb**, <u>not</u> to annoy motorists but to:

  -avoid drains, potholes and debris

  -be seen as they come to junctions with side roads

  -discourage drivers from squeezing past where it's too narrow

4 Cyclists **turning right are exposed** - and need extra consideration from motorists, especially on multi-lane roads with fast-moving traffic.

5 Cyclists **can be forced into faster traffic** - by vehicles parked in cycle lanes, at junctions or on double yellow lines.

6 Cyclists **are dazzled** by full-beam headlights, like everyone else.

7 Cyclists **can be fast movers** - 20mph or more.

www.safespeed.org.uk

LEARNING TOGETHER:
Research And Create Your Own Leaflet

Next, you are going to research and create your own leaflet.

TASK 1

Bring in some leaflets for your group to read. You will find these in many places including hospitals, shops, restaurants, museums and cinemas. Advertising leaflets often come through the letterbox. Share the leaflets with your group.

After reading through the leaflets, decide which ideas, layouts or other features you would like to include in your own leaflets.

TASK 2

Now create your own leaflet. The purpose of your leaflet could be to explain something – for example, 'How to look after your goldfish'. Or it could be to give information – for example, about 'One Direction' or 'Famous Scottish Inventions'. It's up to you.

TASK 3

Put all the leaflets that everyone in your class or group has produced in a pile. Everyone should choose two leaflets at random and read them. What are the differences and similarities between them? Which do you prefer and why? Find out who has written the leaflets and share your ideas with them both.

ONLINE

Watch the clip at http://www.bbc.co.uk/education/clips/z7qvr82. Phil is writing an article for a BMX magazine – he gives you useful information about how to build up an opening paragraph.

ONLINE

These links give lots more information about factual writing/information leaflets:
-http://www.bbc.co.uk/education/clips/z7qvr82
-http://www.bbc.co.uk/bitesize/standard/english/close_reading_texts/newspapers_information_leaflets/revision/2/

How To Look After Your Goldfish

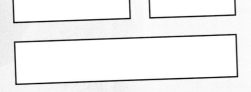

One Direction

THINGS TO DO AND THINK ABOUT

Start to look for examples of really clear, well-written leaflets (and those that are not so clear and well-written!) and bring them in for your group or class to analyse and evaluate.

DON'T FORGET

Remember that audience and purpose are very important when we read *and* when we write. (Look back to pages 14 and 15 for information about audience and purpose.) Who will need your leaflet? Is it aimed at experts or beginners? Is it meant to be read by other pupils or adults, too?

DISCURSIVE WRITING 1

WHAT IS DISCURSIVE WRITING?

Discursive writing:

- is about a topic or issue
- includes evidence such as facts, information and statistics.

The main purpose of discursive writing is to:

- put forward arguments for and/or against a topic
- persuade the reader.

PERSUASIVE AND ARGUMENTATIVE WRITING

There are two main types of discursive writing. In **persuasive** writing, you write in favour of one side of an argument. In **argumentative** writing, you explain both sides of the argument.

Discursive writing often appears in magazines and newspapers. For example, you might read an article about why a motorway should **and** should not be built through the rural area where you live: the writer is looking at **both** sides of the argument.

Then again, you might read an article in a health magazine giving you lots of reasons why you should eat less sugar: in this case, the writer of this article only looks at **one** side of the argument.

 **ACTIVITY**

Look at the table below. It contains discursive essay titles. Work out from the title whether the essay is persuasive (one side of the argument only) or argumentative (looking at both sides). One example has been done for you.

Title	Persuasive or argumentative?
Why animal cruelty is wrong	
State schools vs private schools	
Plastic surgery – good or bad?	
Ban advertisements on social networks!	
Online shopping is killing the high street	Persuasive

WRITING FRAMES

Did you know that some people believe that American astronauts did **not** land on the moon in 1969? Others believe that they did land on the moon.

- If you are writing a **persuasive** essay about the moon landings, you will explain why you think they did happen **or** why you think they did not happen.
- If you are writing an **argumentative** essay about the moon landings, you will explain why you think they did happen **and** why you think they did not happen.

It is important to organise both types of essay very clearly. There are two frames on the next page to help you with this. A writing frame is a 'skeleton' or framework that you can fill in.

OPINION PHRASES

In persuasive writing, you should include your own opinions, so you need to use words and phrases such as:

- Obviously ...
- In my view ...
- My opinion is ...
- Clearly ...
- I think/believe that ...
- Personally ...
- As far as I am concerned ...

LOOKING AT EXAMPLES 1

You are going to look at two examples of persuasive writing – a letter and an essay.

 **LEARNING TOGETHER:** Letter

We'll look at the letter first.

Read the following letter through carefully.

> Sir, I am getting increasingly annoyed at the barrage of articles about teenagers and the adults who keep trying to explain our behaviour...
>
> I am 16 and a straight-A student, like most of my friends. We are not as irrational and immature as adults seem to think ...
>
> Has no one ever seen that we are angry at the world we live in? Angry that we will have to clean up your mess ...
>
> I would like adults to treat us not as strange creatures from another world but as human beings with intelligent thought ...
>
> Stop teaching adults to behave around us, and instead teach them to respect us.
>
> Jenni Herd
>
> (Adapted from http://www.thetimes.co.uk/tto/opinion/letters/article4021903.ece)

Try writing a **one-sentence** summary of Jenni's letter. Now share your sentence with others in the group – discuss all the sentences you have written. Use the best ideas from the group to create the best one-sentence summary.

 ## THINGS TO DO AND THINK ABOUT

Jenni obviously feels strongly about the way adults treat teenagers. If there is an issue you feel strongly about, why not blog about it? There is a simple guide on how to start blogging at http://startbloggingonline.com/

DISCURSIVE WRITING 4

LOOKING AT EXAMPLES 2

The second example is an essay about the 'glass ceiling'. Essays usually contain a bibliography, so it's important that you know what this is and what it should contain.

BIBLIOGRAPHY

A bibliography is an alphabetical list of all the sources you have read/watched/used for your essay. Here is the information to include in your bibliography:

Text/source	Information needed
Book	Author(s), title, publisher, date of publication
Film	Director, title, date of release
TV programme	Title, director, channel, date of broadcast
Radio programme	Title, director, radio station, date of broadcast
Newspaper or magazine article	Author, title, date of publication
Website	Full address, date you accessed the website

 LEARNING TOGETHER: Reading An Essay

Read the following essay carefully, and think about whether it is persuasive or argumentative.

Is the 'Glass Ceiling' Cracking?

This essay will discuss the glass ceiling which is a term referring to women not being able to get into senior/better paid jobs. It means that senior jobs are hard for women to reach. This essay will discuss the glass ceiling and I will reach a conclusion about whether the glass ceiling is breaking or not.

The glass ceiling exists because there is a gender pay gap. The gender pay gap means that women are paid less than men. Some statistics show that on average women earn 23% less than men. 80% of women are in lower paid jobs meaning only 20% are in middle and senior management. The higher up the ladder you climb, the bigger the pay difference – female directors earn an average salary of £127257 which is £14689 less than men in the same jobs. This evidence all shows that the gender pay gap still exists.

Women are rarely found in upper management positions. There are very few women in high profile jobs such as lawyers, judges, doctors and top-level managers and executives. Women have an average 30.9% of the most senior positions in business, politics and police. The armed forces and the law have the fewest women in top posts – 1.3% and 13.2% – while secondary education has the most (36.7%). Men outnumber women by four to one in Parliament. According to a BBC News report in 2012, women represent 1.3% of the highest positions in the Army, Navy and RAF, 13.2% of the most senior judges, 14.2% of university vice-chancellors, 16.6%

of the most senior staff in the police and 34.7% of the senior civil service. However, the European Commission is considering new laws to get more women into the top management jobs which will help to break the glass ceiling.

Many jobs are considered to be 'female' jobs. This means people think these jobs are more suitable for women than men. Typical jobs for women include secretaries, child care, teaching assistants, housekeeping and cleaning, hairdressers, teachers, nurses and shop assistants. These jobs are thought of as more suitable for part time work because many women want to look after under-school age children and cannot work fulltime. Women working in jobs such as plumbing, scaffolding, fire-fighting and rubbish collecting will help to break this stereotype.

In conclusion, there have been some improvements for women recently like the move towards equal pay for women and men. But as long as people stereotype women, the glass ceiling will always exist.

Bibliography

http://www.bbc.co.uk/news/uk-18187449 accessed 5.5.2014
http://www.theguardian.com/business/2013/jan/06/overlooked-underpaid accessed 6.5.2014
http://www.prospects.ac.uk/equality_and_diversity_women.htm accessed 6.5.2014

TASK 1

With your partner, look for examples of evidence that the writer uses to back up the statements she makes. One paragraph has been done for you in this way – the statement is highlighted in green and the evidence is highlighted in red. How many examples of evidence can you find in the other paragraphs?

TASK 2

Now it's over to you to write an essay. Choose your topic, do your research, use a frame and off you go!

You can choose a topic from the list below if you want:

- Should school start later in the morning?
- Do violent films make teenagers violent?
- Should animals be used to test cosmetics?
- Should boys and girls be taught separately in single sex schools?
- Are zoos cruel?
- Should school cafeterias offer healthy food options only?
- Cheap fashion – is it worth the price?
- Should overweight passengers pay more for transport?

ONLINE

You could also watch and listen to the film called *Should Children be Banned From Watching TV?* at www.bbc.co.uk/education/clips/z69vcdm. This film will give you lots of information to use in an essay. You can write a persuasive essay or an argumentative essay – it's up to you. Or choose a topic of your own – again, it's up to you.

When everyone has finished their essays, mark your partner's work and give them some feedback. Use green pencil to underline what has been done well (for example, you could underline a great word or a clear explanation) and a red pencil to underline something that could be improved. Remember to include a comment to explain the reasons for your underlining.

ONLINE

There is lots of helpful advice about discursive writing at http://www.bbc.co.uk/education/guides/zn64jxs/revision

THINGS TO DO AND THINK ABOUT

Take some time to look back over this chapter. Remember that you were asked to assess your writing skills at the beginning of the chapter? What do you think about them now? Answer as honestly as you can.

Red means that you find the skill challenging (or are unsure what it means). Amber means that you need more practice in the skill. Green means that you are confident in the skill.

Writing skills	Red	Amber	Green
I can use appropriate ideas.			
I can use appropriate language.			
I can use appropriate structure.			
I write clearly so that someone else can understand my writing.			

Make an 'action plan' to identify any aspect of writing that you still want to work on:

Action	My plan
Area for improvement – for example, organisation	My area for improvement is...
Action – for example, revise, ask teacher for help, practise more	I am going to...
Learning target – for example, to improve my organisation of writing	This will improve...

KEY SKILL – TALKING

TALKING IN NATIONAL 4 ENGLISH

The focus in this chapter is on the skill of talking. Talking is one of the skills (or Outcomes) in the Creation and Production Unit. It is also one of the skills (or Outcomes) in the Literacy Unit. To achieve a pass in Talking (in English **and** Literacy) at National 4 level, you have to show that you can talk to communicate.

This chapter will help you to:

- choose ideas to use when you are talking
- choose language to use when you are talking
- organise what you say – for example, when you are giving a talk
- use non-verbal communication such as body language.

The chapter is divided into two sections – the first section is about group discussion and the second section is about individual talk.

Lots of the advice will be the same – for example, it is important that you speak clearly whether you are in a group or talking individually.

TALKING: WHAT SKILLS WILL I DEVELOP?

The Outcome and Assessment Standards for talking in the Creation and Production Unit and in the Literacy Unit are shown side-by-side in the table below.

	Creation and Production Unit	Literacy Unit
Outcomes	2 Participate actively in straightforward spoken activities by:	4 Talk to communicate, as appropriate to audience and purpose, by:
Assessment Standards	2.1 Selecting ideas and content, using a format and structure appropriate to purpose and audience 2.2 Applying knowledge of language in terms of language choice 2.3 Communicating meaning at first hearing 2.4 Using aspects of non-verbal communication	4.1 Selecting and using straightforward language 4.2 Organising spoken communication 4.3 Using non-verbal conventions

TALKING OUTCOMES AND ASSESSMENT STANDARDS EXPLAINED

So, to pass National 4 English, you need to show that you can do the following:

CHOOSE APPROPRIATE IDEAS

This means your ideas have to 'fit' the context. For example, talking in a group discussion at a pupil council meeting where everyone is speaking formally and taking turns is very different to the way you speak when you are arguing with your friends about which café you want to go to after school!

CHOOSE WORDS AND PHRASES THAT ARE APPROPRIATE FOR THE CONTEXT

If you were having a job interview, you would use different words and phrases to those you would use with your friends or a family member.

ORGANISE WHAT YOU SAY

This can mean using a clear structure with an introduction and a conclusion if you are giving an individual talk. It can also mean taking turns during a group discussion.

COMMUNICATE MEANING AT FIRST HEARING

This means that what you say has to make sense to whoever is listening.

USE NON-VERBAL COMMUNICATION

This means using eye contact, facial expression, pace, intonation and gesture. There's much more on this later in the chapter.

HOW AM I DOING?

Before you begin, think about how you rate your talking skills and fill in the grids below. **Red** means that you find the skill challenging (or are unsure what it means). **Amber** means that you need more practice in the skill. **Green** means that you are confident in this skill.

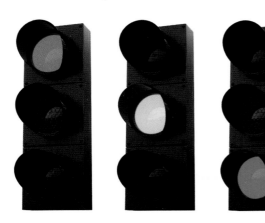

GROUP DISCUSSION

Talking skills – group discussion	Red	Amber	Green
I can choose what ideas I will use in the discussion.			
I can use language to suit the purpose of the group discussion.			
I can organise what I say			
I can communicate clearly.			
I can use body language and eye contact.			

INDIVIDUAL TALK

Talking skills – individual talk	Red	Amber	Green
I can choose ideas for my talk.			
I can use language to suit the purpose of my talk and my audience.			
I can organise my talk – for example, I can use an introduction and conclusion.			
I can communicate clearly.			
I can use body language and eye contact.			

 **DON'T FORGET**

Answer as honestly as you can! If you find this difficult, ask your teacher for some feedback about how you are doing in group discussion and individual talk.

THINGS TO DO AND THINK ABOUT

We are going to start by thinking about group discussions. Use this checklist when you are listening to yourself or to others in a group discussion:

Did I/they:	Group member 1	Group member 2	Group member 3	Group member 4
Listen to others?				
Take turns to speak?				
Contribute ideas?				
Ask questions				
Develop what others said?				
Challenge others?				
Check understanding?				
Summarise what was said?				

GROUP DISCUSSION 1

TAKING PART IN GROUP DISCUSSION

The types of group discussion you might have could be:

- a group interview for a job
- a discussion with a group of friends
- a discussion at a pupil council meeting
- a family discussion about where to go on holiday.

LEARNING TOGETHER:
Rules For Group Discussion!

Take part in a group discussion to agree on five 'rules' for your discussions. It might be helpful to think about the statements below. Use them to start off your discussion.

- You can interrupt, as long as you are polite.
- It's rude not to join in.
- Listening means being silent.

Here are three 'rules' that one group has come up with. Your group could start off by talking about these or changing them. Then add another two rules.

ROLES IN GROUP DISCUSSION

Roles are the 'jobs' we have in a group. Sometimes you will choose which role to have and sometimes your teacher will tell you your role.

There are other roles in group discussion but we will concentrate on these three.

Look over the table below to see what each role is. Think about what you could do and say in these roles:

Group Rules

1. Everyone in the group should listen to the others' ideas and opinions.
2. Everyone in the group should get the chance to speak.
3. No-one in the group should talk all the time.
4.
5.

Role	What you can do	What you can say
Leader	<ul><li>Pays attention and is on task</li><li>Introduces the discussion</li><li>Encourages each group member to contribute</li><li>Contributes ideas</li><li>Is open to new ideas</li></ul>	'Today, we have to decide ...' 'Who agrees with Eve about ...?' 'Let's get back to the task ...' 'What do you think, Amir?' 'Is our final decision that ...?'
Recorder/ reporter	<ul><li>Pays attention and is on task</li><li>Notes down what people say in the discussion</li><li>Reports back on what the group decided/talked about</li></ul>	'Did you say that ...?' 'Do you want me to report back that ...?' 'What is our decision about...?'
Time-keeper	<ul><li>Pays attention and is on task</li><li>Tells the group how much time it has</li><li>Tells the group how much time is left – for example, half way through</li><li>Tells the group when time is up</li></ul>	'We have ten minutes left ...' 'We should decide now ...'

CONTRIBUTING TO DISCUSSION

All group members should:

- pay attention and stay on task
- listen to others
- take turns to speak
- contribute ideas
- ask questions
- develop what others say – for example, by giving an example or agreeing/disagreeing
- challenge others if appropriate
- check understanding
- summarise what has been said.

Look at the questions and statements on the next page. Highlight one question or statement in each box to use in your next group discussion.

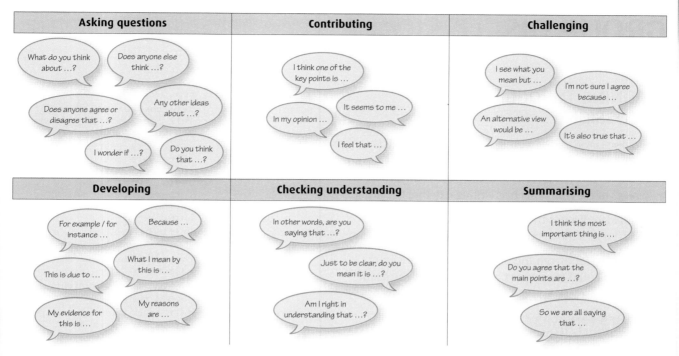

ACTIVITY: Watch And Listen To A Discussion

You are going to watch and listen to a discussion. First, look at the ten statements below. These are all statements you will hear in this discussion. Now decide if each of the following statements shows that someone is **agreeing with**, **disagreeing with** or **developing** the discussion (for example, by adding something or by contributing an idea). When you've done that, put each statement into the correct box. One of each type has already been done for you.

ONLINE

Now watch and listen to the discussion at http://www. educationscotland.gov.uk/ learningteachingand assessment/assessment/ssln/ resources/literacydiscussion new/literacydiscussionsupport/ skillsmakingcontributions.asp. The group is discussing the reasons why youths commit crime after reading the novel *Holes*. You can pause and listen to the discussion as many times as you want.

Agreeing with the discussion	Disagreeing with the discussion	Developing the discussion
I think parental responsibility is a great point ...	I kind of disagree because...	going back to what Ali said a minute ago about...

THINGS TO DO AND THINK ABOUT

Carry out some research so that you know a few facts about youth crime. For example:

- What is youth crime?
- At what age, on average, do young people start to commit crimes?
- Is youth crime increasing?
- What types of crimes do young people commit?

- Do more young boys than young girls commit crimes?
- What are the reasons for young people committing crimes?

GROUP DISCUSSION 2

LEARNING THROUGH GROUP DISCUSSION

Group discussion can be a great way of learning. This is because you can learn from others, especially if you keep an open mind. You can discuss topics like youth crime as well as aspects of the course such as writing together in a group.

You can also discuss the texts you read in National 4 English, so let's move on to a group discussion of fiction.

Read this extract from the play *The Steamie* by Tony Roper. You could take a part or even act out the scene if you want.

 **LEARNING TOGETHER:**
Group Discussion 1

Discuss the characters in this extract and how they treat each other. One comment has been included to start you off.

- Dolly –
- Magrit – is sarcastic towards Mrs Culfeathers.
- Mrs Culfeathers –
- Doreen –

LEARNING TOGETHER:
Group Discussion 2

Let's start by thinking about how teenagers are actually talking less nowadays!

'Hey'   'whats up?'   'idk'   'L'   'later'   'kl'
Text messaging is now the most popular method of communicating. We use our phones for text messaging far more often than for phone calls.

What are some of the advantages of texting?

- Perhaps you want to be private – phone calls can be overheard.
- Texting means you have time to think about exactly what you want to include in your message.
- You can text lots of your friends at once by sending a group text.

What are some of the disadvantages of texting?

- Texting means you are not paying attention to the world around you.
- Texting means you are not aware of the person's body language or reactions.
- A text is forever! You may write something rude or unpleasant which can't be deleted.

DOLLY:	Wait tae ye hear this. Tell them what ye telt me Mrs Culfeathers.
MRS CULFEATHERS:	Well I wis tellin' Dolly that I aye got ma mince oot o' Galloways because it is lovely mince . . . there's hardly any fat in their mince Doreen ye know.
DOREEN (slightly mystified):	Aye, oh, it's good mince.
MRS CULFEATHERS:	D'ye no like their mince Magrit?
MAGRIT:	Aye . . . it's awright. (Looks at DOLLY.)
DOLLY:	Tell them aboot whit Mr Culfeathers says aboot it.
MRS CULFEATHERS:	Well . . . I wis tellin' Dolly aboot how I aye get ma mince oot o' Galloways, but sometimes I get it oot another butchers . . . ye know just for a wee change, and I was saying that when I get it oot another butchers, Mr Culfeathers can always tell, even though I havenae said whit butcher's I got it oot o'. If I pit mince doon tae him, and I havenae got it oot o' Galloways, he aye says tae me, 'where did ye get that mince fae?'
MAGRIT (slight sarcasm):	Does he? . . . (To DOREEN) D'ye hear that?
DOREEN:	Aye . . . that's . . . that's . . . that's eh . . . very interesting.
MRS CULFEATHERS:	That shows ye what good mince it is.
DOLLY:	Oh it is . . . aye it is good mince, isn't it Magrit?
MAGRIT:	Oh . . . second tae none.
DOLLY:	But that's no the end o' it. There's mair.
DOREEN:	Surely not.
MAGRIT:	Ye mean even mair interesting than that?
DOLLY:	Aye . . . wait tae ye hear this.
MAGRIT:	Well I don't see how you can top that but do go on …

Extract taken from *The Steamie*, by Tony Roper. Play text published in *Scot-free: New Scottish Plays*, edited by Alasdair Cameron (Nick Herne Books, 1990).

TASK 1

Choose **one** of the activities below for your group/team:

Discuss the advantages and disadvantages of texting in your group and come to a decision about texting. Overall, is it good or bad?

or

In your group, decide which device you would miss most if you were forced to live without technology!

TASK 2

This next group discussion is about stereotypes. (Look up 'stereotype' in a dictionary and share what you find out.)

On your own, write a list of all the Scottish stereotypes you can think of. Include clothing, behaviour, sayings and characteristics usually associated with Scottish people – for example, wearing kilts, drinking whisky and eating haggis!

In your group, share your lists and choose the ideas you like best. Create one group list from these and discuss the following questions:

- What does your list tell you about Scottish people and Scotland?
- Where have these ideas come from? Is there any truth in these ideas?
- Have you ever been stereotyped? Where, when and why?

BOUNCING

Have you heard of 'bouncing' in group discussion? This is a way of making sure everyone is involved. Practise bouncing during your group discussion about stereotypes by using each others' names.

- 'I like Kyle's idea but what do you think, Ian?'
- 'Matt, do you agree with Holly?'
- 'I disagree with Mo – Cayleigh, can you back me up?'

ONLINE

Edward de Bono created a way of thinking in group discussions that might help you. Look at the coloured hats approach at www.debonothinkingsystems. com/tools/6hats.htm

LEARNING TOGETHER:
Fist-To-Five

You can use 'fist-to-five' to check out how everyone's feeling about the discussion. Each person shows a fist or a number of fingers as follows:

Fist	I need to discuss this a lot more.
1 Finger	I still need to discuss some things and I want to suggest changes we could make.
2 Fingers	I am comfortable with the idea but would like to discuss some more about it.
3 Fingers	I don't agree completely but I feel OK with the idea/decision.
4 Fingers	I agree with it.
5 Fingers	I think it's a great idea/decision.

It's a good idea to stop every five minutes or so to use 'fist-to-five'. When everyone in the group shows more than three fingers, the decision is made and the group can move on.

DON'T FORGET

Use the checklist on page 81 to evaluate your group discussions.

THINGS TO DO AND THINK ABOUT

It is a great idea to film your group discussion! Watch the film so you can comment on yourself or watch someone else so that you can comment on how well they did.

INDIVIDUAL TALK 1

This section of the chapter will help you develop your skills in individual talk. An individual talk can also be called an 'individual presentation' or just a 'presentation'.

Think about when you might give a talk or presentation. This could be:

- giving a talk for one of your school subjects
- talking about yourself at a job interview
- giving a presentation at assembly
- making a speech at a ceremony.

This section will help you with how to:

- choose what to say in your talk
- use appropriate language in your talk
- organise your talk
- communicate clearly
- use non-verbal communication effectively.

QUICK TALKS

Try one of the quick talk activities below.

ACTIVITY: Two Truths And A Lie

Tell the rest of your group/class two truths and one lie about yourself. For example, 'I have one brother, I have been to Ibiza and I play the trumpet'. The others have to guess which are the truths and which is the lie.

ACTIVITY: Just A Minute

Play the 'Just a Minute' game. You have 60 seconds to talk about a topic without hesitating and without repeating a word or phrase. Either present your talk to the rest of the group or the whole class. Your teacher will give you topics to choose from, or you can choose from the list below:

- my favourite breakfast
- the best way to travel
- ghosts
- how others see me
- pop music

DON'T FORGET

Before you start, look back at the self-assessment table on page 81 to check how well you perform in individual talks.

ACTIVITY: I've Never …

Everyone stands in a circle. One person says something he or she has never done – for example, 'I've never eaten salmon'. Everyone who has **done** that thing (that is, everyone who has eaten salmon) then steps into the centre of the group. The game continues until every person has said something they've never done and everyone is in the centre.

ACTIVITY: 30 Seconds

Form two circles – one inside the other – so you have an inner circle and an outer circle. People in the inner circle pair up face-to-face with partners from the outer circle. These partners share their ideas about a topic for 30 seconds each. For example, if the topic is 'My worst nightmare', one person describes this for 30 seconds, then the next person and so on.

After each of these talk activities, think about the following:

- How easy/difficult was it?
- What went well?
- What would you do differently next time?

ACTIVITY: Body Language

Watch and listen to a talk by McKenna Pope at www.ted.com/talks/mckenna_pope_want_to_be_an_activist_start_with_your_toys

Turn the sound down so that you cannot hear what McKenna says. You are watching her body language – the way she uses her facial expression and her body (for example, her hands) – to support what she says.

ONLINE

Listen to a podcast of the 'Just a Minute' BBC Radio 4 programme at www.bbc.co.uk/programmes/b006s5dp to hear how it is played.

TASK 1

First of all, think about and write down your thoughts on McKenna's body language. Now share these with your partner. Use the table below to comment. One has already been done for you. Be prepared to share your ideas with the rest of the group/class.

Body language	Your comment
Eye contact	Looks directly at audience
Hands	
Movement	
Facial expression	

Here are some top tips for body language:

	What to do	Ideas for practice
Facial expression	Smile while you talk. (This helps make you look confident even if you are not feeling confident!) Use facial expressions (for example, surprise, excitement) to suit what you are talking about.	Practise talking in front of a mirror – this is the only way you can know what people see when you are talking to them! You could practise using different expressions.
Movement	Don't fidget, shuffle or bite your nails! Try to stand or sit still – use your hands if you wish, for example, to point something out or to emphasise what you are saying.	Practise talking in front of a mirror – this is the only way you can know what people see when you are talking to them! You could practise using different expressions.

McKenna's talk is about how she convinced Hasbro, one of the world's biggest toy companies, to change the way that they marketed a toy kitchen. One of the purposes of her talk is to tell her audience about what she did and how she felt about what she achieved. Then her purpose changes – she tries to persuade you to change things even if people criticise you.

TASK 2

Now turn up the volume and listen to McKenna's talk. Answer the questions below about the volume, pace and tone of her talk.

	Question	Your comment
Volume	Is McKenna's voice too loud, too soft or just right?	
Pace	Does Mckenna speak too slowly, too fast or just right?	
Tone	Does Mckenna speak in one dull tone or does she vary her tone (using high and low voice)?	

Here are some top tips for volume, pace and tone:

	What to do	Ideas for practice
Volume	Speak clearly and loudly – make sure you are speaking loudly enough so you can be heard. Ask at the beginning 'Can everyone hear me?'	Practise speaking loudly enough by getting a partner to listen to you at the back of a large hall – for example, your school hall. Can they hear you?
Pace	Don't speak too fast or too slow!	Time yourself so that you get the pace just right. How much can you say in one minute, speaking clearly and steadily?
Tone	Use your voice to make your talk interesting. If you talk in the same tone all the time, your audience will be bored.	Try making the most important words in a sentence 'stand out' by making your voice higher when you say these words. Try making your voice rise and fall.

THINGS TO DO AND THINK ABOUT

Choose your favourite TV or radio presenter. Think about the volume, pace and tone that they use. What two stars and a wish (remember the feedback sandwich on page 69) would you give this person about the volume, pace and tone of what they say?

INDIVIDUAL TALK 2

USING APPROPRIATE LANGUAGE

Listen to Tom Leonard reading his poem *Unrelated Incidents – No.3* at http://www.bbc.co.uk/education/clips/z42g9j6.

Unrelated Incidents – No.3

this is thi
six a clock
news thi
man said n
thi reason
a talk wia
BBC accent
iz coz yi
widny wahnt
mi ti talk
aboot thi
trooth wia
voice lik
wanna yoo
scruff. if
a toktaboot
thi trooth
lik wanna yoo
scruff yi
widny thingk
it wuz troo.
jist wanna yoo
scruff tokn.
thirza right
way ti spell
ana right way
to tok it. this
is me tokn yir
right way a
spellin. this
is ma trooth.
yooz doant no
thi trooth
yirsellz cawz
yi canny talk
right. this is
the six a clock
nyooz. belt up.

LEARNING TOGETHER:

Informal Words And Phrases

This poem is written as it sounds (this is called phonetic spelling). The poem contains lots of informal words. Think individually and write down five informal words and phrases from the poem. Now work with your partner and share your words. Work out how these could be expressed formally. Complete the table below. One example has been done for you. Be prepared to share your ideas with the rest of your group/the class.

Informal word/phrase	Formal word/phrase
'belt up'	'Please be quiet'

ONLINE

Watch and listen to the Armstrong and Miller sketch at https://www.youtube.com/watch?v=IlYyL0y5QY4. Can you work out why the way these pilots talk is so funny?

ONLINE

Watch the film clip at www.bbc.co.uk/bitesize/ks3/english/speaking_listening/speaking/activity/ which shows an actor called Jeremy using formal and informal language. Click to show when Jeremy is using formal language and when he is talking informally. You can replay the clip if you need to.

LEARNING TOGETHER:
Giving A Presentation

TASK 1

Read the online newspaper *The Day* at www.theday.co.uk. Choose any article that interests you and discuss it with your partner. What article did you choose and why? Be prepared to share your ideas with the rest of your group/the class.

DON'T FORGET

You can read the poem as you listen to Tom Leonard. Or, if you prefer, read it to a partner yourself!

TASK 2

You are going to give a presentation on a topic that is based on your chosen article. For example, if you chose an article about an increase in the number of stray dogs in Scottish towns, you could talk about animal cruelty, the SSPCA or any other topic related to the article. There are some more examples below:

Headline		Suggested topics
'Orkney islands at risk of global warming'		-Global warming -The environment -Island life
'Falkirk Kelpies celebrate 15000 visitors in first two months'		-My town/community -Art/architecture -Landscape
'World Cup shame – player takes drugs test'		-Football -Sport -Drugs in sport
'Nelson Mandela greatest leader according to poll'		-Nelson Mandela -South Africa -Heroes/heroines

TASK 3

Once you have chosen your topic, start preparing your presentation. Write your topic in the middle of a page and create a mind map around it.

Think about:

- What do you think or feel about your topic?
- Have you any relevant experiences you could talk about?
- Where can you find more information – for example, facts and figures – about your topic?
- Where can you find illustrations, diagrams or objects to illustrate your talk?

If you choose a topic such as 'drugs in sport' or 'South Africa', you will have to carry out research so that you have information to include in your talk. When you have plenty of ideas on your mind map, decide which of these ideas you want to include in your presentation. You could use a highlighter to choose these.

You should put the main ideas or headings on to small cards (these are called cue cards). Look at this example:

Introduction – introduce myself and topic – 'What I like best'

Cue card 1 – I like doing gymnastics – give reasons – keeps me healthy and strong – love jumping/somersaults/tumbles – great club – good friends – fun

Cue card 2 – I like being with my family – walking with dog – describe dog – where we go – feeling of being together

Cue card 3 – I like art – favourite thing – drawing/painting – reasons – fun – never boring – love using different paints/pencils – gallery in my room

Conclusion – Love all three – favourite is gymnastics – thanks for listening – any questions?

TASK 4

Practise, practise, practise. Then test out your speech on a friend or family member. How successful was it? How long did it take? Ask for feedback on how to improve your talk.

THINGS TO DO AND THINK ABOUT

Use humour in your talk if this feels natural for you. You could tell a funny story or start your talk with a relevant joke. And whether you include humour or not, don't forget to smile at your audience!

89

INDIVIDUAL TALK 3

ORGANISATION

Think about how to organise your talk. The simple structure used for the gymnastics talk on page 89 is:

- Introduction
- Interest 1
- Interest 2
- Interest 3
- Conclusion

The order for your talk is up to you. Remember, though, that you must always include an introduction and a conclusion.

In your **introduction**:

Introduce yourself	My name is Ashia
Greet your audience	Hello/good morning/welcome
State clearly what you are going to talk about	I'm going to talk about how we should treat older people ...
State your purpose clearly	I'm going to explain why I think we should treat older people with respect and look up to them ...

In your **conclusion**:

State clearly what you have talked about	I've been talking about respect for older people ...
Thank audience	Thank you for listening ...
Invite questions	Does anyone have a question?

VISUAL AIDS

You can use visual aids to make your talk more interesting. For example, you could bring in a map to show the audience if you are talking about your town. Think about the best visual aids for your topic – you might not be allowed to bring your pet rabbit into school, but you could bring photographs or pictures of it! If you are talking about a news article, why not show a copy of the article to the audience?

Visual aids include:

- whiteboard/blackboard
- video clip
- flipchart
- paper handout
- slide show
- objects

⚙ ACTIVITY: Change A Well-Known Story

Try telling a story you know really well, but introduce some key changes. For example, we all know the story of Cinderella. You could tell the story to a partner or a group, but with the following differences:

- Change names, gender, objects or places – for example, Cinderella could be called 'Arabella', the ugly sisters could be brothers, the slipper could be a tiara and so on.
- Change the plot of the story – for example, have a different ending.

Practise using visual aids when you tell your 'new' Cinderella story. There are lots to choose from – you could use slides, show objects (such as a tiara!), show a film clip and so on.

⚙ ACTIVITY: Quick Talks

Now practise your talking skills with one of these quick and easy ideas. Choose the one that appeals to you most and talk to your group or class about it:

- Talk about a teacher you like/admire and why
- Talk about the best book you have ever read
- Talk about a person who supports you
- Talk about something you feel proud of
- Describe something you love doing
- Describe your favourite thing to do at the weekend
- If you could have three wishes, what would they be?

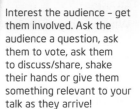
DON'T FORGET

Interest the audience – get them involved. Ask the audience a question, ask them to vote, ask them to discuss/share, shake their hands or give them something relevant to your talk as they arrive!

ASSESSING YOUR TALK

Use this checklist yourself when you are giving a talk, or when you are listening to someone else give a talk.

ONLINE

Did you know there is an International Talk like a Pirate Day? Check out www.talklikeapirate.com/howto.html

Speaker's name _____	Yes/no	Comment
Was there an introduction?		
Were the ideas interesting?		
Was the talk well organised?		
Did the speaker speak loudly enough?		
Did the speaker speak at the right pace?		
Did the speaker use visual aids?		
Did the speaker speak clearly?		
Was there a conclusion?		
Did you enjoy the talk?		

THINGS TO DO AND THINK ABOUT

Take some time to look back over this chapter.

At the beginning of this chapter, you were asked to assess your talking skills? What do you think about them now? Answer as honestly as you can.

Red means you find the skill challenging (or are unsure what it means). Amber means that you need more practice in the skill. Green means that you are confident in the skill.

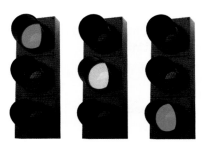

Talking skills – individual talk	Red	Amber	Green
I can choose what ideas I will put in my talk.			
I can use language to suit the purpose of my talk and my audience.			
I can use appropriate structure such as using an introduction and conclusion in my talk.			
I can communicate clearly.			
I can use body language, eye contact and other features of non-verbal communication.			

Talking skills – group discussion	Red	Amber	Green
I can choose what ideas I will use in group discussion.			
I can use language to suit the purpose of the group discussion.			
I can use appropriate structure.			
I can communicate clearly.			
I can use body language, eye contact and other features of non-verbal communication.			

Make an 'action plan' to identify any aspect of talking you still want to work on:

Action	My plan
Area for improvement – for example, eye contact	My area for improvement is...
Action – for example, revise, ask teacher to help, practise more	I am going to...
Learning target – for example, to improve my eye contact when I am talking	This will improve...

THE ADDED VALUE UNIT

THE ASSIGNMENT: STEP BY STEP 1

INTRODUCTION

To pass National 4 English, you must complete an Added Value Unit. This is an assignment, which uses all four of your language skills – reading, listening, writing and talking.

To complete the Added Value Unit you will:

- choose and plan your assignment
- carry out and record your research
- show your understanding of two texts (at least one of the texts must be written)
- evaluate these two texts
- present your ideas
- answer questions about the topic.

Your assignment will be either written (a 700–800 word essay) or spoken (a four to six minute individual talk to a group of at least three people).

Here are the Outcome and the Assessment Standards for the National 4 English Added Value Unit:

National 4 English Added Value Unit		
Outcome	1.	Apply language skills to investigate a chosen topic by:
Assessment Standards	1.1	Understanding and evaluating straightforward texts
	1.2	Selecting relevant information from the texts
	1.3	Presenting findings on the topic
	1.4	Responding to oral questions relevant to the topic

ASSIGNMENT OUTCOMES AND ASSESMENT STANDARDS EXPLAINED

To pass the Added Value Unit, you will use reading, listening, talking and writing to:

- understand and evaluate at least two texts, using appropriate technical terms
- find ideas in the texts that are relevant to your assignment
- write or talk about what you have found out
- answer questions about what you have found out.

HOW AM I DOING?

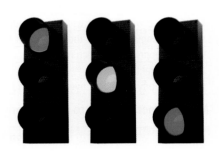

Before you begin, think about the language skills you will need for your assignment and fill in the grid below. Answer as honestly as you can!

Red means that you find the skill challenging. **Amber** means that you need more practice in the skill. **Green** means that you are confident in the skill.

Language skills	Red	Amber	Green
I can understand and evaluate texts.			
I can select relevant ideas from texts.			
I can write or talk about my ideas.			
I can answer questions about my ideas.			

Step 1	Choosing your assignment
Step 2	Choosing your focus
Step 3	Note-taking
Step 4	Selecting information
Step 5	Evaluating
Step 6	Presenting your ideas
Step 7	Responding to questions

YOUR STEP-BY-STEP GUIDE TO THE ASSIGNMENT

The best way to approach your assignment is to work through it using the steps to the right. Your teacher will give you advice about how to record what you do, how and where to keep the information you find and when the deadlines are for each step.

STEP 1 – CHOOSING YOUR ASSIGNMENT

The first step is to choose which type of assignment you want to do. You could choose to:

- write a critical essay (or give a presentation) about fiction texts
- write a critical evaluation (or give a presentation) about non-fiction texts.

We'll look in detail at both types of assignment so that you understand what is involved in each type. This will help you to make an informed decision about which assignment is best for you.

You must write about **at least** two texts. Most pupils choose to study two texts, so this is the approach we will use in this chapter. If you want to write about more than two texts, talk to your teacher about how you might do this.

DON'T FORGET

If you write about fiction, you could choose:
-a film
-a novel
-TV drama
-poetry
or any other fiction text.
Discuss this with your teacher!

CRITICAL ESSAY

If you choose to write a critical essay (or give a presentation) about two fiction texts, you will need to:

- choose two texts that are connected in some way – for example, on the same theme or written by the same author
- explain why you have chosen these texts
- show that you understand the ideas/information in these texts
- evaluate an aspect(s) of the texts
- write an equal amount about each of the texts
- select at least one **written** text – for example, a novel. The other text can be a written text, a digital text or a media text.

There are two approaches to this type of assignment. The table below gives you an example of each approach:

Approach	Suggested texts	Example
You could read two texts and write (or talk) about the similarities and differences between them. This is called 'comparing and contrasting'.	A novel and a film	Read the short novel *The Body* by Stephen King and compare and contrast it with the film *Stand By Me* which is adapted from this novel.
You could read two texts and write (or talk) about them separately.	Two short stories	Read two short stories – *Tinsel* by Alan Spence and *All That Glisters* by Anne Donovan – and write/talk about them.

Your two texts can be from the same genre – for example, two poems, or they can be from different genres – for example, a play and a poem.

THINGS TO DO AND THINK ABOUT

TOP TIPS

- Choose texts that you have enjoyed or found interesting.
- Remember that you need to evaluate at least two texts.
- Choose texts that you can find out about – for example, from online research.
- Know your texts very well.
- Choose this type of assignment if you feel confident writing/talking about literature.

THE ASSIGNMENT: STEP BY STEP 2

STEP 1 – CHOOSING YOUR ASSIGNMENT (CONTINUED)

CRITICAL EVALUATION

If you choose to write a critical evaluation (or give a presentation) about two non-fiction texts, you will need to:

- choose two texts that are connected – for example, they are about the same issue or topic
- explain why you have chosen these texts
- show that you understand the ideas/information in these texts
- evaluate an aspect(s) of the texts
- write an equal amount about each of the texts
- select at least one written text – for example, a book. The other text can be a written text, a digital text or a media text.

There are two approaches to this type of assignment. The table below gives you an example of each approach:

Approach	Suggested texts	Example
You could read two texts and write (or talk) about the similarities and differences between them. This is called 'comparing and contrasting'.	Two magazine advertisements	Read two magazine advertisements and compare and contrast them.
You could read two texts and write (or talk) about them separately.	A newspaper article and a website	Read a newspaper article and a website about teenage fashions and write/talk about them separately.

Your two texts can be from the same genre – for example, two travel brochures, or they can be from different genres – for example, a website and a newspaper article.

TOP TIPS

- Choose a topic that you find interesting and want to know more about.
- Remember that you need to evaluate at least two texts – for example, a documentary film and a book about your topic.
- Choose a topic that you can find out a lot about – for example, from online research.
- Know your texts very well.

DON'T FORGET

You have a wide choice of non-fiction texts to choose from including:
-biography
-autobiography
-TV documentary
-travel writing
-reference books
-podcast.

STEP 2 – CHOOSING YOUR FOCUS

Once you have chosen your topic and your texts, the next step is to choose an aspect or the aspects you will focus on. Your focus will depend on whether you have chosen to read fiction or non-fiction texts.

It is a good idea to include this focus in the title for your assignment/presentation – look at the examples below, which are based on the suggestions on the page 93.

Write a critical essay (or give a presentation) about fiction texts		
Texts	**Suggested focus**	**Suggested title**
Read the short novel *The Body* by Stephen King and compare and contrast it with the film *Stand By Me* that is adapted from this novel.	Similarities and differences between characters and plot in the book and the film.	'A Comparison of the Characters and Plot in *The Body* and *Stand By Me*'
Read two short stories – *Tinsel* by Alan Spence and *All That Glisters* by Anne Donovan – and write/talk about them separately.	*Tinsel* – how the writer develops a believable main character. *All That Glisters* – how the writer develops a believable main character.	'The Main Characters in *Tinsel* and *All That Glisters*'

There are lots of other aspects you could choose to write or talk about, depending on what texts you have chosen. If you are writing or talking about fiction, you could write about:

- language
- characters
- setting
- theme
- plot

Write a report (or give a presentation) about non-fiction texts		
Texts	**Suggested focus**	**Suggested title**
Read two magazine advertisements and compare and contrast them.	Similarities and differences in the information, language and layout of the advertisements.	'A comparison of two car advertisements'
Read a newspaper article and a website about teenage fashions and write/talk about them separately.	How persuasive the newspaper article is. How persuasive the website is.	'Persuasive techniques in *What Teens Ought Not To Wear* and at www.teenstalkfashion.com'

There are lots of other aspects you could choose to write or talk about, depending on what texts you have chosen. If you are writing/talking about non- fiction, you could write about:

- language/style
- layout/format
- information
- writer's techniques.

 ### LEARNING TOGETHER:
Choosing Your Texts, Focus And Title

TASK 1

Take plenty of time to choose your texts, focus and title. Share your ideas with your partner and ask for feedback. They should then do the same for you. Be prepared to share your ideas with the rest of your group/class, too.

My texts	My focus	My title
Feedback:	Feedback:	Feedback:

DON'T FORGET

Talk to your teacher about which aspect(s) you want to choose. It is important to get feedback at each stage.

Act on any feedback and revise your texts, focus or title as appropriate. Take your time. You will probably go through several choices before you finally decide.

TASK 2

You are going to present your texts, focus and title to other learners. Your purpose is to persuade your group (or the whole class) that your assignment is the best.

In your presentation, you will include your draft title, the texts you have chosen and why, your focus and the skills you are going to show in your assignment.

DON'T FORGET

Your purpose is to persuade. You could use some of the techniques you learned about on page 76 to make your presentation stand out from the rest.

 ### THINGS TO DO AND THINK ABOUT

Remember to:

- speak clearly
- be confident – no one knows more about your assignment than you do!
- be prepared for any questions you might be asked.

Task 2's short presentation will be good practice if you are going to present your final assignment orally. Good luck!

THE ASSIGNMENT: STEP BY STEP 3

STEP 3 – NOTE-TAKING

Try to find out as much as you can about your texts. Do you know anyone – for example, a teacher, a librarian or a family member – who could tell you more about them? Think about all the sources you could use to find information:

- books
- magazines
- newspapers
- television programmes/documentaries
- radio programmes/podcasts
- films
- websites/blogs/wikis.

Once you've got information about the texts, you need to remember it. And you also need to remember the ideas and information within the texts themselves. Taking notes will help you to do this.

When you take notes on a text, always make a note of the title, the author, the publisher and the date of publication.

SUMMARISING

Summarising means giving an outline of the main points in a text. This is a very useful skill when note-taking. Look at the following 'dos and don'ts' of summarising.

Do:

- use key words and phrases from the text
- use your own words
- use mind-maps/diagrams/pictures

Don't:

- copy out whole sentences
- include examples

Remember that you can also annotate texts you read. Annotation means adding notes to a text to comment or explain something in the text. You can annotate by highlighting, underlining or adding notes in the margin or within the text itself. This means you will have to print out texts such as a poem or a page from a website, or you could buy your own copy of a text.

DON'T FORGET

You can take notes in lots of ways. Some people prefer to make visual diagrams such as flow charts or mind-maps. It's up to you. The best way to take notes is in a way that makes sense to you.

DON'T FORGET

Top tips for note-taking
-Don't just copy everything you read or write down, or everything you watch or listen to – only write down key points/words.
-Use your own words whenever possible.
-Use sections, headings, underlining and bold to highlight points and make your notes easier to understand later.

LEARNING TOGETHER   Note-Taking

TASK 1

Read the short news article entitled 'Horse sculptures trot in to boost visitors to Hamilton' on page 9 again.

Lucy has read this article and has used a mind-map to create notes.

Murray has read this article and has written some notes.

Fraser has read this article and annotated it.

Look at their work on page 97:

ASSIGNMENT WRITING/TALKING – STRUCTURE 2

Paragraph/section	Advice
Introduction	Include details of texts (titles, authors, dates) and state your focus clearly.
Paragraph/section 1	Text 1 – explain what the text is and why you chose it. Give information about the text.
Paragraph/section 2	Make one point about Text 1 – show your understanding of the text and evaluate it with evidence.
Paragraph/section 3	Make one point about Text 1 – show your understanding of the text and evaluate it with evidence.
Paragraph/section 4	Make one point about Text 1 – show your understanding of the text and evaluate it with evidence.
Paragraph/section 5	Text 2 – explain what the text is and why you chose it. Give information about the text.
Paragraph/section 6	Make one point about Text 2 – show your understanding of the text and evaluate it with evidence.
Paragraph/section 7	Make one point about Text 2 – show your understanding of the text and evaluate it with evidence.
Paragraph/section 8	Make one point about Text 2– show your understanding of the text and evaluate it with evidence.
Conclusion	Sum up your overall opinion about the texts.

You might use more paragraphs/sections, depending on your focus.

THINGS TO DO AND THINK ABOUT

Remember to use the PEEL structure for each paragraph/section:

P	POINT	Make a point about your focus
E	EXPLANATION	Explain what this shows/means
E	EXAMPLE/EVIDENCE	Give an example or quote directly from the text to justify your explanation
L	LINK	Your last sentence should link to your next paragraph

Read over the example paragraph below from an assignment which compares the film 'My Fair Lady' and the play 'Pygmalion' by George Bernard Shaw.

Use four different colours of highlighter to highlight:

- the 'point' in the paragraph
- the explanation in the paragraph
- the examples or pieces of evidence in the paragraph
- highlight the 'link' in the paragraph

Eliza's introduction to upper class life means she leaves her impoverished life behind and she begins to realise that Higgins is controlling her as she becomes a lady. 'I have my feelings same as anyone else' suggests that Eliza is starting to become aware of what is happening to her and that she is not a 'toy' for Higgins. Higgins tempts her with 'think of chocolates, and taxis, and gold, and diamonds' and is confident he can 'make a duchess out of this guttersnipe'. However, his wife, Mrs Higgins thinks 'Eliza's not quite ready' and still needs to improve.

Mrs Higgins treats Eliza as...

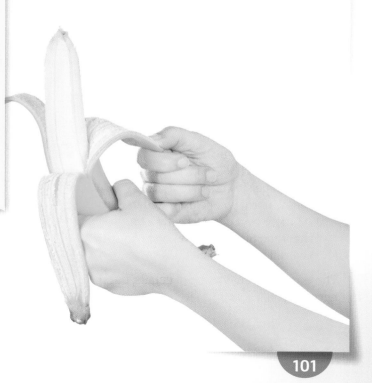

THE ASSIGNMENT: STEP BY STEP 6

STEP 6 – PRESENTING YOUR IDEAS ORALLY

If you are giving an oral presentation, look closely at the advice on page 89 about how to structure a presentation. If you follow this advice, you will know what to say. But **how** are you going to say it? Here are a few ideas.

LENGTH

Remember that your presentation should last 4–6 minutes. You can prepare for your presentation by practising in front of family or friends. Get to know how much you can say in 4–6 minutes. It's actually quite a long time so you need to have more than one or two ideas!

USING CUE CARDS

You can use cue cards (small 'flash cards' where you can write headings, words or bullet points) to help you remember what to say.

USING VISUAL AIDS

In your presentation, you could use visual aids such as:

- slides
- film clips
- a display
- a website
- maps
- diagrams
- photographs
- pictures
- objects
- models.

If you use presentation software:

Do	Don't
Use a large clear font	Use small font
Use only a few words on each slide	Write lots of information on each slide
Use a clear layout – for example, bullet points	Use too many colours or designs

MAKING YOUR TALK MORE ENGAGING

You can make your talk more engaging by:

- using music or sound as part of your presentation
- including a question(s) to ask the audience or even a quiz for them to do in advance.

PRACTISE, PRACTISE, PRACTISE!

Find out the following information in advance:

- Where will you give your presentation – at the front of the classroom or perhaps in another school space?
- Will you be sitting or standing?
- What you will you be expected to wear?
- Will there be a desk or lectern for you?
- What time of day will you be giving your presentation?
- Who will the audience be?

These might seem like small details, but the more you prepare and plan, the less nervous you will be.

ONLINE

If you want to use slides during your presentation, think about using prezi (www.prezi.com) or Zoho show (www.zoho.com) as an alternative to PowerPoint. Or you could use another type of visual aid such as a flip chart or a whiteboard.

DON'T FORGET

On the day of your presentation, get your visual aids ready in advance and make sure all your IT is working.

A WORD ABOUT NERVES ...

It is natural to feel nervous about speaking in front of an audience. Even the most famous presenters and interviewers admit they still get nervous!

Always take your time at the beginning of a presentation if you are nervous. For example, take your time to smile at the audience and to introduce yourself. It's not a race! Breathe in slowly a couple of times and then start off when you are ready.

Breathe deeply, drink water (have a glass or bottle of water beside you during your talk) and try to talk at a normal pace. Most of us speed up if we are nervous, so be aware of this and slow down if you can.

Always finish strongly and thank your audience for listening. Ask if they have any questions. Keep smiling!

DON'T FORGET

There is a whole chapter on talking earlier on in this Study Guide. Look back at the section on pages 86-91 about 'Individual talk' – this will help you if you are giving a talk for your assignment.

STEP 6 – PRESENTING YOUR IDEAS IN WRITING

If you are writing your presentation, here are a few ideas:

LENGTH

Remember that you should write 700–800 words. Get to know what 700–800 words looks like. How many pages will this be if you handwrite it? If you are word-processing your essay, it is easy to use the word count to keep track of length.

ORGANISATION AND EXPRESSION

All the usual rules about writing apply: use paragraphs, check your spelling and punctuation and make sure your sentences make sense. Turn back to the 'Key skill – writing' chapter earlier in the Study Guide for lots more advice.

DON'T FORGET

You can write your presentation **or** give a talk. Your teacher will tell you more about which one you will do.

DRAFTING AND REVISING

Keep asking for feedback so that you can keep improving your writing. Refer to the advice on drafting and proofreading in the chapter on writing.

STEP 7 – RESPONDING TO QUESTIONS

You will be expected to respond to questions about your assignment.

For example, you might be asked:

- Why did you choose this topic/these texts?
- What did you know about this topic/these texts already?
- What did you want to find out?
- What did you find out?
- Which text(s) did you prefer and why?
- What have you learned from the texts?
- Would you recommend the texts to others and why?

Remember to answer the questions you are asked with as much detail as you can.

 ## THINGS TO DO AND THINK ABOUT

Your teacher will tell you when you will answer these questions. You might do this earlier on in the process – for example, during your research – or at the end – for example, after your presentation.

EXAMPLE APPROACHES

Here are three different approaches to the assignment.

APPROACH A

Hannah has chosen to write a critical essay about fiction texts.

Hannah has decided to compare a book and a film – her favourite book of all time is *The Fault in our Stars*!

Her focus is on the two main characters (and how they are similar/different in the book and the film) and on a key scene (and how it is different in the book and the film).

Draft title	'A comparison of the novel *The Fault in Our Stars* with the film of the same name'
Introduction	Hannah gives background information about the novel and author, the film and director and explains why she chose them. She explains her focus.
Paragraph 1	Hannah gives a brief summary of the setting, plot and the main characters.
Paragraph 2	Hannah explains how Hazel is portrayed in the book and the film, and how the portrayals are similar. She gives evidence and quotes from both texts.
Paragraph 3	Hannah explains how Hazel is portrayed in the book and the film, and how the portrayals are different. She gives evidence and quotes from both texts.
Paragraph 4	Hannah explains how Augustus is portrayed in the book and the film, and how the portrayals are similar. She gives evidence and quotes from both texts.
Paragraph 5	Hannah explains how Augustus is portrayed in the book and the film, and how the portrayals are different. She gives evidence and quotes from both texts.
Paragraph 6	Hannah explains what happens in a key scene – Hazel and Gus' visit to the Anne Frank House. She evaluates how this is presented in the book with evidence and quotes.
Paragraph 7	Hannah evaluates how this scene is presented in the film (with evidence and quotes) and explains which she thinks is better and why.
Conclusion	Overall, Hannah sums up what she thinks about the book and the film. She explains that she thinks the book is better than the film with an explanation/evidence for why she thinks this.

If you want to compare a book and a film, here are some other suggestions:

- *The Boy in the Striped Pyjamas* by John Boyne
- *The Hunger Games* by Suzanne Collins
- *The Great Gatsby* by F Scott Fitzgerald
- *Coraline* by Neil Gaiman
- *The Lord of the Flies* by William Golding
- *To Kill a Mockingbird* by Harper Lee
- *The Twilight Saga* by Stephanie Meyer
- *Holes* by Louis Sachar

APPROACH B

Cameron has decided to give a presentation about two non-fiction texts.

Cameron has two cats at home and enjoys looking after them and reading about how to care for them.

He evaluates how effectively information is presented in *Complete Cat Care* and *The Cat Care Book* in his log book, recording his evaluation comments.

He decides to focus on the content, language and layout of both texts in his final presentation.

Draft title	'A comparison of two texts about caring for cats'
Introduction	Cameron gives background information about the books and why he has chosen them. He explains his focus.
Section 1	Cameron gives a brief explanation of the content, language and layout used in the two texts.

Section 2	Cameron explains what information is included in *Complete Cat Care* and *The Cat Care Book*. He gives evidence and quotes from both texts.
Section 3	Cameron comments on the language in *Complete Cat Care* and *The Cat Care Book*. He gives evidence and quotes from both texts.
Section 4	Cameron talks about the layout of *The Cat Care Book* and *Complete Cat Care*. He gives evidence and quotes from both texts.
Conclusion	Overall, Cameron sums up what he has learned from both books, with an explanation/evidence for why he thinks this.

If you want to compare non-fiction texts, here are some suggestions:

- leaflets/brochures
- reference books
- factual websites
- TV documentaries

- biography
- autobiography
- travel writing

APPROACH C

Stevie has decided to write a critical evaluation about two non-fiction texts.

Stevie has decided to write about school uniform because his school is about to introduce a school dress code.

One text he has read is a newspaper article arguing that school uniform is a good idea – 'School Uniform Improves Results'. He has also read an online news article against school uniform – 'The Freedom to Wear what You Want'.

He decides to focus on how effective the texts are in persuading him about school uniform.

Draft title	'School Uniform – am I persuaded for or against?'
Introduction	Stevie gives background information about the articles and why he has chosen them. He explains his focus.
Paragraph/section 1	Stevie gives a brief explanation of the arguments in article 1.
	Stevie gives a brief explanation of the arguments in article 2.
Paragraph/section 2	Stevie explains how the main argument in article 1 is much clearer than the main argument in article 2. He gives evidence and quotes from both texts.
Paragraph/section 3	Stevie explains how the examples given in article 1 are much more persuasive than in article 2. He gives evidence and quotes from both texts.
Paragraph/section 4	Stevie explains how the school statistics/results in article 2 are much more persuasive than in article 1. He gives evidence and quotes from both texts.
Paragraph/section 5	Stevie explains how the language in article 1 is much more persuasive than in article 2. He gives evidence and quotes from both texts.
Conclusion	Overall, Stevie explains which article he finds more persuasive and why.

If you want to compare issue-based texts, you could read:

- factual websites
- news articles
- magazine articles

- books
- leaflets/brochures

 THINGS TO DO AND THINK ABOUT

Take some time to go back over these three approaches, and then decide which of them is:

- the most interesting, and why?
- the most challenging, and why?

Share your decision and reasons with your partner. Be prepared to share your ideas with the rest of the group/class.

LEARNING LOG 1

THINKING ABOUT YOUR PROGRESS

Take some time to look back over this chapter. Remember that you were asked to assess your language skills at the beginning of the chapter. What do you think about them now? Answer as honestly as you can.

Red means that you find the skill challenging (or are unsure what it means). **Amber** means that you need more practice in the skill. **Green** means that you are confident in this skill.

Language skills	Red	Amber	Green
I can understand and evaluate texts.			
I can select relevant ideas from texts.			
I can write or talk about my ideas.			
I can answer questions about my ideas.			

Make an 'action plan' to identify any aspect of your assignment you still want to work on:

Action	My plan
Area for improvement – for example, organisation	My area for improvements is...
Action – for example, revise, ask teacher for help, practise more	I am going to...
Learning target – for example, to practise talking to an audience	This will improve...

ADDED VALUE UNIT: LEARNING LOG

You have to keep a learning log as you work through your assignment step by step so you won't forget what you have done and where you are. There is an example of a learning log on pages 107–109.

DON'T FORGET

You can use or adapt this example, or you can use a different learning log. Talk to your teacher about how to record your learning.

THINGS TO DO AND THINK ABOUT

Take a break and review where you are with your assignment after you have completed steps 1 to 4.

Reflect on the following:

- How well are you doing with your assignment (how do you know?)
- What you have done so far?
- What you have found out so far?
- How well have you learned so far, and why?
- What have you found easy or difficult, and why?
- What have you liked (or disliked) about the learning?
- What would you do differently next time?
- Anything else you can think of about your learning so far.

Make sure you are:

- keeping your bibliography/list of sources up to date
- asking for help if you need it
- clear about what you still have to do.

STEP 1 – CHOOSING YOUR ASSIGNMENT

All the texts/websites I have considered are _____

The title of text 1 I have chosen is _____

The author of text 1 is _____

Publisher/date of publication/ISBN number _____

I chose this text because _____

The title of text 2 I have chosen is _____

The author of text 2 is _____

Publisher/date of publication/ISBN number _____

I chose this text because _____

STEP 2 – CHOOSING YOUR FOCUS

1. I will focus on _____

2. My draft title is _____

STEP 3 – RESEARCHING AND NOTE-TAKING

Some ideas and evidence I have noted from text 1 are:

Some ideas and evidence I have noted from text 2 are:

LEARNING LOG 2

STEP 4 – SELECTING INFORMATION

The key ideas and evidence from text 1 are:

[ ]

The key ideas and evidence from text 2 are:

[ ]

STEP 5 – UNDERSTANDING AND EVALUATING

Notes on the effectiveness of text 1:

[ ]

Notes on the effectiveness of text 2:

[ ]

STEP 6 – PRESENTING YOUR IDEAS

Written assignment

I have chosen to write my assignment because _____

The deadline for my final draft is _____

Spoken assignment

I have chosen to make a presentation because _____

I am going to use visual aids including _____

The date for my presentation is _____

STEP 7 –DRAFTING YOUR ASSIGNMENT

Written assignment

I have completed my first draft (date) _____

I have completed a self-evaluation on my first draft _____

Feedback comments from my partner on my first draft are _____

Feedback comments from my teacher on my first draft are _____

In my final draft, I am going to _____

Spoken assignment

I have done a practice talk (date) _____

I have completed a self-evaluation on my practice talk _____

Feedback comments from my partner on my practice talk are _____

Feedback comments from my teacher on my practice talk are _____

In my final presentation, I am going to _____

STEP 8 — RESPONDING TO QUESTIONS

I might be asked _____

I could respond by saying _____

I have practised my responses by _____

GLOSSARY

Alliteration
repeating sounds at the beginnings of words/ phrases, such as 'tempting and tasty on toast!', used to create an effect.

Assonance
the repetition of a certain group of similar-sounding vowels in words close to each other, such as 'now brown cow', again used to create a certain effect.

Autobiography
when somebody describes their own life story and achievements, the author is talking about themselves so they use 'I', 'me' and 'my'.

Biography
when the story of a person's life is told by somebody else. In biographies, the author will use 'he/she', 'him/her' and 'his/her'.

Character
a person represented in a ~v.

~h are very
'e 'roses

End rhyme
rhyming words at the end of lines, such as:
Humpty Dumpty sat on a wall, Humpty Dumpty had a great fall

Format
the arrangement of a text. If it is a television show, the format could mean panel debate or interview show. In a written text, the format could mean a report or a short story.

Hyperbole
using exaggeration to emphasise, for example 'the list goes on for miles'.

Imagery
language used to create images in the reader's mind, such as 'The juicy tomato burst in her mouth'.

Intonation
making words louder or quieter for emphasis, think about the different intonation that could be put on 'I don't agree!'

Internal rhyme
use of rhyming words within a line, such as:
Double, double toil and ~ouble, Fire burn and
'~on bubble

'hich we all
~ading,

Personification
describing an object as if it were a person, such as 'the fire raged'.

Plot
the story of a text. The plot covers all of the action in the story.

Repetition
repeating a word or phrase, for example 'Believe in yourself and you will go far. Believe. Believe in yourself and the sky's the limit.'

Rhetorical question
questions expecting no direct answer, rather the reader's support for the writer's views. Who wants to see a child suffer in this way? Here the reader is expected to share the writer's horror at the ill-treatment of children.

Rhyme
the pairing of words with the same sound, used usually in poetry.

Rhythm
the pattern of sounds created by syllables in a line/ verse, such as:
I wandered, lonely as a cloud...

Rule of three
using three words or ideas or numbers to highlight a particular point, for example 'education, education, education'

~rison of two things
~e' or 'as'. For
'hair like gold'.

~m
~g the opposite of what ~neant, for example 'My good friend, the traffic warden.'

Setting
the time and/or place in which a story happens. For example, John Steinbeck's Of Mice and Men is set in California during the Great Depression.

Structure
the way in which parts of a text are organised or arranged.

Style
how a writer creates effects in his or her work by, say, imagery, word choice, tone, anecdote, sentence structure or any other features which mark a writer's unique voice.

Theme
a central idea that binds together characters or situations in a novel or short story. It is what the text is about. For instance, the theme of loneliness is explored in John Steinbeck's Of Mice and Men.

Travel writing
texts including outdoor literature, exploration literature, adventure literature, mountain literature, nature writing, and the guide book, as well as accounts of visits to foreign countries.

Word choice
the writer's decision to use certain words to show an effect or a tone. For instance, does he/she refer to a woman as 'slim' or 'scrawny'? The word chosen will indicate his/her attitude to the woman in question, i.e. elegant and trim, or underweight to the point of being unattractive.

Writer's techniques
the way in which a writer has chosen to present their text. Writer's techniques include alliteration, imagery and rhyme.

~ey
~plash!'